D1528365

MARCH ONTO LAND

THE SILURIAN PERIOD TO
THE MIDDLE TRIASSIC EPOCH

THE PREHISTORIC EARTH

Early Life:
The Cambrian Period

The First Vertebrates:
Oceans of the Paleozoic Era

March Onto Land:
The Silurian Period to the Middle Triassic Epoch

Dawn of the Dinosaur Age:
The Late Triassic & Early Jurassic Epochs

Time of the Giants:
The Middle & Late Jurassic Epochs

Last of the Dinosaurs:
The Cretaceous Period

The Rise of Mammals:
The Paleocene & Eocene Epochs

The Age of Mammals:
The Oligocene & Miocene Epochs

Primates and Human Ancestors:
The Pliocene Epoch

Early Humans:
The Pleistocene and Holocene Epochs

THE PREHISTORIC EARTH

MARCH ONTO LAND

THE SILURIAN PERIOD TO THE MIDDLE TRIASSIC EPOCH

Thom Holmes

CHELSEA HOUSE
PUBLISHERS
An imprint of Infobase Publishing

THE PREHISTORIC EARTH: March Onto Land

Chelsea House
An imprint of Infobase Publishing
132 West 31st Street
New York NY 10001   JUL 2 2 2008

Library of Congress Cataloging-in-Publication Data

Holmes, Thom.
    March onto land / Thom Holmes.
        p. cm. — (The prehistoric Earth)
    Includes bibliographical references and index.
    ISBN 978-0-8160-5959-1 (hardcover)
    1. Vertebrates, Fossil—Study and teaching—United States. 2. Geology, Stratigraphic—Triassic.
I. Title. II. Series.

    QE841.H655 2008
    560—dc22   2007045330

CONTENTS

PREFACE

To be curious about the future one must know something about the past.

Humans have been recording events in the world around them for about 5,300 years. That is how long it has been since the Sumerian people, in a land that today is southern Iraq, invented the first known written language. Writing allowed people to document what they saw happening around them. The written word gave a new permanency to life. Language, and writing in particular, made history possible.

History is a marvelous human invention, but how do people know about things that happened before language existed? Or before humans existed? Events that took place before human record keeping began are called *prehistory*. Prehistoric life is, by its definition, any life that existed before human beings existed and were able to record for posterity what was happening in the world around them.

Prehistory is as much a product of the human mind as history. Scientists who specialize in unraveling clues of prehistoric life are called *paleontologists*. They study life that existed before human history, often hundreds of thousands and millions of years in the past. Their primary clues come from fossils of animals and plants and from geologic evidence about Earth's topography and climate. Through the skilled and often imaginative interpretation of fossils, paleontologists are able to reconstruct the appearance, lifestyle, environment, and relationships of ancient life-forms. While paleontology is grounded in a study of prehistoric life, it draws on many other sciences to complete an accurate picture of the past. Information from the fields of biology, zoology, geology, chemistry, meteorology, and even astrophysics is called into play to help the paleontologist view the past through the lens of today's knowledge.

If a writer were to write a history of all sports, would it be enough to write only about table tennis? Certainly not. On the shelves of bookstores and libraries, however, we find just such a slanted perspective toward the story of the dinosaurs. Dinosaurs have captured our imagination at the expense of many other equally fascinating, terrifying, and unusual creatures. Dinosaurs were not alone in the pantheon of prehistoric life, but it is rare to find a book that also mentions the many other kinds of life that came before and after the dinosaurs.

The Prehistoric Earth is a series that explores the evolution of life from its earliest forms 3.5 billion years ago until the emergence of modern humans some 300,000 years ago. Four volumes in the series trace the story of the dinosaurs. Six other volumes are devoted to the kinds of animals that evolved before, during, and after the reign of the dinosaurs. *The Prehistoric Earth* covers the early explosion of life in the oceans; the invasion of the land by the first land animals; the rise of fishes, amphibians, reptiles, mammals, and birds; and the emergence of modern humans.

The Prehistoric Earth series is written for readers in middle school and high school. Based on the latest scientific findings in paleontology, *The Prehistoric Earth* is the most comprehensive and up-to-date series of its kind for this age group.

The first volume in the series, *Early Life*, offers foundational information about geologic time, Earth science, fossils, the classification of organisms, and evolution. This volume also begins the chronological exploration of fossil life that explodes with the incredible life-forms of the Precambrian and Cambrian Periods, more than 500 million years ago.

The remaining nine volumes in the series can be read chronologically. Each volume covers a specific geologic time period and describes the major forms of life that lived at that time. The books also trace the geologic forces and climate changes that affected the evolution of life through the ages. Readers of *The Prehistoric Earth* will see the whole picture of prehistoric life take shape. They will learn about forces that affect life on Earth, the directions that life can sometimes take, and ways in which all life-forms depend on each other in the environment. Along the way, readers also will meet many of the scientists who have made remarkable discoveries about the prehistoric Earth.

The language of science is used throughout this series, with ample definition and with an extensive glossary provided in each volume. Important concepts involving geology, evolution, and the lives of early animals are presented logically, step by step. Illustrations, photographs, tables, and maps reinforce and enhance the books' presentation of the story of prehistoric life.

While telling the story of prehistoric life, the author hopes that many readers will be sufficiently intrigued to continue studies on their own. For this purpose, throughout each volume, special "Think About It" sidebars offer additional insights or interesting exercises for readers who wish to explore certain topics. Each book in the series also provides a chapter-by-chapter bibliography of books, journals, and Web sites.

Only about one-tenth of 1 percent of all species of prehistoric animals are known from fossils. A multitude of discoveries remain to be made in the field of paleontology. It is with earnest, best wishes that I hope that some of these discoveries will be made by readers inspired by this series.

—Thom Holmes
Jersey City, New Jersey

ACKNOWLEDGMENTS

I would like to thank the many dedicated and hardworking people at Chelsea House. A special debt of gratitude goes to my editors, Brian Belval and Frank Darmstadt, for their support and guidance in conceiving and making *The Prehistoric Earth* a reality. Frank was instrumental in fine-tuning the features of the series as well as accepting my ambitious plan for creating a comprehensive reference for students. Brian greatly influenced the development of the color illustration program and supported my efforts to integrate the work of some of the best artists in the field, most notably John Sibbick, whose work appears throughout the set.

I am privileged to have worked with some of the brightest minds in paleontology on this series. Ted Daeschler of the Academy of Natural Sciences in Philadelphia reviewed the draft of *March Onto Land* and made many important suggestions that affected the course of the work. Ted also wrote the Foreword for the volume.

The excellent copyediting of Mary Ellen Kelly was both thoughtful and vital to shaping the final manuscript and I thank her for her valuable review and suggestions.

In many ways, a set of books such as this requires years of preparation. Some of the work is educational, and I owe much gratitude to Dr. Peter Dodson of the University of Pennsylvania for his gracious and inspiring tutelage over the years. Another dimension of preparation requires experience digging fossils, and for giving me these opportunities I thank my friends and colleagues who have taken me into the field with them, including Phil Currie, Rodolfo Coria, Matthew Lammana, and Ruben Martinez. Finally comes the work needed to put thoughts down on paper and complete the draft of a book, a process that always takes many more hours than I plan on. I thank Anne for bearing with my constant state of busy-ness and for helping me remember the important things in life. You are an inspiration to me. I also thank my daughter, Shaina, the genius in the family and another inspiration, for always being supportive and humoring her father's obsession with prehistoric life.

FOREWORD

Only in hindsight can we recognize a series of evolutionary changes as truly significant in the history of life. For example, only by looking back in time from the perspective of what we know today can we comprehend that the ability of plants and animals to live on land was hugely consequential to the diversity and distribution of life on Earth. In crossing the barriers of living in water to living on land, plants and animals took a step that would open a major new chapter in the history of life. If the cascade of evolutionary changes that enabled life to invade land had not taken place during the Silurian and Devonian Periods, life on earth may have remained only in the seas, where it had been for the preceding 2 billion years or more.

In Thom Holmes's *March Onto Land*, we see the power of evolution to adapt living things for the new ecological opportunities in semiterrestrial or terrestrial habitats. The evolution of life onto land is also an excellent example of the interconnectedness of life: As one group evolves to better fit new conditions, it creates new opportunities for other groups. Thus, these coevolutionary processes are constantly at work, creating connections between all parts of the ecosystem. Holmes develops this idea within the first section of this book, The Greening of the Paleozoic World, with his examination of plants and arthropods, the true pioneers of terrestrialization. In large part, these organisms created the physical and biological setting that were the crucible for the origin of limbed vertebrates during the latter part of the Paleozoic.

Many discoveries of the earliest limbed vertebrates (early tetrapods) and their closest ancestors among the lobe-finned fishes have been made in recent years. Thom Holmes has endeavored to present the latest discoveries and the most recent analyses of the growing body of fossil evidence concerning the evolutionary transition from fish to tetrapod that occurred in the late part of the Devonian Period. Holmes discusses recent fossils bearing on this question that have been discovered from locations around the world, including my own experiences in the wonderfully rugged terrain on Canada's Nunavut Territory. You will learn that many of the features we associate with limbed animals, including the basic skeletal structures within limbs, first appeared within the lobe-finned fish. In fact, although it seems counterintuitive, the earliest limbed animals were primarily aquatic, suggesting that rudimentary limbs evolved for use in shallow water and swampy habitats. Only after many millions of years, during which these early tetrapods developed specialized structures in the limbs and other parts of the body, did they free themselves from dependence on watery habitats.

In Section Three of *March Onto Land,* Thom Holmes surveys the early amniotes, fully terrestrial tetrapods from the Carboniferous (Pennsylvania and Mississippian) and Permian Periods. This diverse assemblage demonstrates a great range of specializations to living on land—a classic adaptive radiation in which a variety of innovations such as the amniote egg and improved limb structure opened up myriad new ecological opportunities in growing terrestrial habitats. Finally, with a review of the major amniote lineages, *March onto Land* lays the foundation for any future discussion of the reptilian groups that dominate terrestrial and marine habitats during the Mesozoic.

As one who specializes in the study of Paleozoic vertebrates, I often hear the opinion that "nothing interesting has happened since the Paleozoic." Indeed, vertebrate life made fundamental strides during the Paleozoic. I hope that this book introduces you to many fascinating fossils and helps make clear how and why life evolved as it has. The principles and processes that determined the early evolution of life continued into the Mesozoic and Cenozoic Eras and to the present day, making the history of life on Earth a great odyssey that we share with all other living things. No wonder every fossil is so interesting!

—Dr. Ted Daeschler
Academy of Natural Sciences
Philadelphia, Pennsylvania

INTRODUCTION

The Cambrian **Period** of the Paleozoic **Era** is known for its remarkable explosion of multicelled **organisms** with hard shells and **exoskeletons**. The **evolution** of early life during the Cambrian set into motion an arms race between **predator** and prey that has continued to escalate over the ages with each new **species** of organism.

From the roots of life in the Cambrian arose the first animals with backbones—the vertebrates. In the vast Paleozoic oceans, fishes of many kinds became the focus of a biological drama that led to their dominance of the world's saltwater and freshwater habitats. Several kinds of Paleozoic fishes such as the sharks and the ray-finned fishes have prospered since their origins more than 400 million years ago. Interestingly, it was a less successful group of fishes, the lobe-finned fishes, that gave rise to the first land vertebrates some 360 million years ago.

WHEN LIFE FIRST EXPLORED NEW OPPORTUNITIES ON LAND

During the late part of the Devonian Period, from about 380 million to 360 million years ago, something remarkable happened. A certain group of fishes developed legs and other key features that would eventually enable them to leave the water to become the first land vertebrates. It was an extraordinary turning point in the history of life on Earth because it triggered the evolution of all land vertebrates and led to the eventual appearance of a curious species known as *Homo sapiens*. Vertebrate life out of water was founded entirely on the **adaptations** that arose from a group of big, lazy fish that liked to wallow about in shallow water. The human species is standing on the shoulders of ancestral lobe-finned fishes, and those fishes had the **forelimbs** to prove it.

15

March Onto Land tells the story of the Paleozoic animals that conquered the challenge of living out of the water. After having gained a toehold on dry land, terrestrial vertebrates grew in numbers and diversity to become the most important large-bodied organisms on the planet. All 45,000 species of living vertebrates, including humans, have origins rooted deep in the Paleozoic past.

Making the move to land was a change that required many specialized adaptations over millions of years. How fish led to animals with legs, how those early land animals adapted to breathing out of water, and how land animals diversified as the terrestrial experiment of evolution unfolded is the story of *March Onto Land*. That story leads, in time, to the appearance of the first dinosaurs and their reptilian kin in the Mesozoic Era and to the rise of the mammals, including humans, in the Cenozoic Era.

OVERVIEW OF *MARCH ONTO LAND*

March Onto Land begins with a look at the dramatic geological and climatic conditions of the Paleozoic Era that made living on land possible for vertebrates. This first section is called, fittingly, The Greening of the Paleozoic World. Chapter 1 describes widespread changes to ocean and land environments, including worldwide **climates**, that served as catalysts for the spread of plants and invertebrates and then of vertebrates to terrestrial habitats the world over.

Chapter 2 examines the evolution from oceanborne algae of the first land plants and the gradual greening of terrestrial world habitats. Chapter 3 tells the story of the first land animals—invertebrates such as scorpions, giant millipedes, spiders, and insects. The presence on land of plants and invertebrates made the spread of vertebrates to the land possible by providing abundant oxygen (a plant byproduct), stable habitats formed by the rooting of trees and other plants, and life-sustaining food in the form of plants as well as invertebrates.

Section Two, Vertebrates on Land, consists of two chapters that trace the adaptation of backboned animals for life on land. Chapter 4 explains the various anatomical adaptations required for survival out of water and describes how certain lines of fish evolved into the first four-limbed vertebrates, the **tetrapods**. Chapter 5 takes a close look at specific families of fishes and early tetrapods to illustrate the transition of vertebrates from water to land. As *March Onto Land* was being written, Dr. Ted Daeschler, the scientific consultant for this volume, made headlines when he and his colleagues Neil Shubin and Farish Jenkins announced the discovery of an important new "missing link" in the fossil history of the fish-tetrapod transition. With Ted Daeschler's help, this book features a close look at the discovery—*Tiktaalik*—a key fossil specimen discovered in Late Devonian rocks of the Canadian Arctic.

Section Three of this book is *The Evolution of Early Amniotes*. In Chapter 6, the story of early land vertebrates expands into the evolution of reptiles and their kin. One key anatomical adaptation that freed many vertebrates from oceans, lakes, and streams was the ability to lay their eggs on land. These animals developed a new kind of semipermeable, amniotic egg that could protect the developing embryo from its surroundings. Modern-day egg-bearing vertebrates—the **amniotes**—have their roots in the Paleozoic Era. Mammals, including humans, are also amniotes, although their eggs are developed within the body.

Chapter 7 introduces the major classes of amniotes, including the **Anapsida** (**basal** reptiles and turtles), **Synapsida** (ancestral mammals), **Diapsida** (lizards, crocodiles, snakes, and extinct dinosaurs and their kin), and the **Euryapsida** (extinct marine reptiles and their kin). The evolution and adaptations of these animals are traced through the close of the Paleozoic Era and into the beginning of the Triassic Period. It was also during this span of time that all life on Earth faced the most devastating **mass extinction** event in the fossil record. The Permian-Triassic **extinction** is examined in *March Onto Land* from the standpoint of its effect on terrestrial animals and plants and the ways in which some branches of the vertebrate family tree persisted while others perished.

Each chapter in *March Onto Land* uses an abundance of tables, maps, figures, and photos to depict the life, habitat, and changing evolutionary patterns that affected Paleozoic organisms. Many chapters also include "Think About It" boxes that elaborate on interesting issues, people, and discoveries related to Paleozoic life.

March Onto Land builds on foundational principles of geology, fossils, and the study of life. Readers who would like to refresh their knowledge of certain basic terms and principles in the study of past life may want to consult the Glossary in the back of *March Onto Land*. Perhaps most important to keep in mind are the basic rules that govern evolution: that the direction of evolution is set in motion first by the traits inherited by individuals, or arising from mutations, and then by the interaction of that individual with its habitat. These changes accumulate, generation after generation, and so allow species to adapt to changing conditions in the world around them. As Charles Darwin (1809–1882) explained, "The small differences distinguishing varieties of the same species steadily tend to increase, till they equal the greater differences between species of the same genus, or even of distinct genera." These are the rules of nature that served to stoke the engine of evolution during the Paleozoic and that gave rise to forms of life whose descendants still populate the Earth.

SECTION ONE:
THE GREENING OF THE PALEOZOIC WORLD

1

PALEOZOIC TERRESTRIAL ENVIRONMENTS

The 291 million-year span of the Paleozoic Era began with the radiation of life in the oceans during the Cambrian and Ordovician Periods. After about 99 million years, just before the beginning of the Silurian Period, conditions began to take shape that could support plant and animal life on land. Until then, the terrestrial environments of the Earth had been barren wastes that consisted primarily of soil-less rock incapable of absorbing water. The only signs of life on land were found in near-shore regions where single-celled marine algae and the most rugged lichenlike fungi began to cling to dry land. This was the beginning of a revolution in the transformation of world habitats that led to colonization of the continents.

The rise of land organisms was triggered by dramatic changes to the geology and climate of the Earth. The struggle for survival and the ability to adapt were played out against a backdrop of radical flux in Earth's habitats marked by several devastating mass extinctions. This chapter explores the changing geology and climate of the Paleozoic Earth that created environments suitable for life on land.

THE CHANGING FACE OF THE EARTH

The evolving Paleozoic Earth experienced widespread tectonic disruptions, abrupt swings in global temperature, fluctuating sea levels, and fundamental changes to the makeup of the planet's atmosphere. The era was also marked by long spans of temperate warmth that contrasted with massive glaciations and their chilling effects.

EVOLUTIONARY MILESTONES OF THE PALEOZOIC ERA

Period	Span (Millions of Years Ago)	Duration (Millions of Years)	Organismal Milestones
Cambrian	542 to 488	54	Shelly marine invertebrates; trilobites; nautiloids; archaic mollusks, brachiopods, echinoderms; marine plants; ancestral chordates and vertebrates
Mass extinction			Casualties: brachiopods, conodonts, and trilobites
Ordovician	488 to 443	45	Radiation of marine invertebrates, corals; jawless fishes; first land plants
Mass extinction			Casualties: trilobites, echinoderms, and nautiloids
Silurian	443 to 416	27	Marine invertebrates renew radiation, including reef colonies; diversification of land plants; diversification of arthropods (land and sea)
Devonian	416 to 359	57	Jawed fishes and ammonoids radiate; first insects and land vertebrates; first seeded plants, first large trees, and forests
Mass extinction			Casualties: ammonoids, trilobites, gastropods, reefs, armored jawless fish, placoderms
Carboniferous	359 to 299	60	Radiation of sharks, bony fishes, and lobe-finned fishes; crinoids, blastoids, and bryozoans; amphibians and insects flourish; coal swamps, early reptiles; ferns, seed ferns, and lycopod trees
Permian	299 to 251	48	Bony fishes and sharks diversify; finbacked synapsids and advanced synapsid reptiles; early gymnosperms (conifers)
Mass extinction			Casualties: trilobites, crinoids, bryozoans, brachiopods, ammonoids, and other marine invertebrates; many early reptiles and mammal-like reptiles

The Earth's oceans were its first livable habitats. During the Cambrian and Ordovician Periods, shallow waters, warm seas, and increasingly oxygenated water led to the rapid and spectacular evolution of marine organisms. The Middle Paleozoic is known as the age of fishes, and not surprisingly—it was during that span of rapid diversification of marine vertebrates that the roots of today's cartilaginous and bony fishes were established.

Some of the key components that make up a successful terrestrial **ecosystem** are a stable ground cover of soil and plants, an abundance of water, breathable air, and shelter from **ultraviolet solar radiation.** During the Cambrian and Ordovician Periods, the world beyond the oceans was not inviting to life. This was because there was no land ecosystem to speak of, only barren rocks on the interior portions of the exposed continents. Complicating and governing all of the factors that combine to make up a terrestrial ecosystem were radical changes taking place in the configuration of the Earth's crust. During the Paleozoic Era, tectonic-plate movements dramatically changed the face of Earth's crust.

Continental Drift and Land Forms of the Paleozoic Era

The effects on marine habitats of **continental drift** during the Paleozoic were vast. A discussion of the effects of these same plate movements on terrestrial habitats introduces the concept of the **craton**. A craton is the large, tectonically stable interior of a continent that remains fairly intact over geologic time.

The Paleozoic Era began with the relatively warm Cambrian Period, a carryover from the temperate Precambrian climate that melted glaciers and flooded the world with mineral-rich waters. Much of the land that had been dry during the Precambrian was flooded during the Cambrian by these warm, shallow waters. Lands that would one day make up continents such as North America, Europe, Asia, and Africa were submerged under temperate, shallow seas. By the end of the Cambrian, however, the seas became deeper, and habitats were vastly transformed. This caused many shallow-water, near-shore species to become extinct.

The largest of the Ordovician landmasses was Gondwana; it was located near the South Pole and consisted of land that one day would form Africa, South America, Australia, Antarctica, and

India. The end of the Ordovician Period was a cold span marked by widespread glaciation on the southernmost Gondwana landmass. This decimated large **populations** of marine organisms unable to adapt to the cold.

During the Silurian Period, northern landmasses began to collide, closing the expanses of ocean between them. The pre–North American and pre-Asian landmasses remained largely under water but edged steadily toward one another while pushing back the sea. Sedimentary formations that would shift with the continental plates over time and are now exposed in Scotland, Scandinavia, and northern Europe were being laid down in thick sandy layers south of the equator. It was during this time that plant and animal life made its first significant forays onto land as soil surfaces formed for the first time and created a stable foundation for the spread of plants.

The latter part of the Paleozoic began with a localized Gondwana glaciation in the Early Devonian Epoch. Mountains that would be part of the Appalachians in eastern North America were forming far to the west near the equator. The sites of New York, Beijing, and Paris were still under water. The topography of the continental cratons became increasingly varied in terms of elevation, climate, and the availability of varied habitats.

The Carboniferous Period was a time of much tectonic activity. The northern landmasses continued to collide, forming mountains ranges in what today are the continents of North America and Europe. Inland seas left behind by receding oceans turned into freshwater marshes, lakes, and swamps where plant and animal life began to flourish. This was the time of the great Carboniferous coal forests. The name "Carboniferous" refers to the vast reserves of coal that formed from the fossilized remains of plants and trees of these forests over millions of years. Levels of atmospheric oxygen became the highest in Earth's history, resulting in the rapid expansion and **gigantism** of insects and other land invertebrates as well as some early tetrapods. Even as vast coal swamps spread across Earth's equator, an ice cap formed across the South Pole. Most of Central

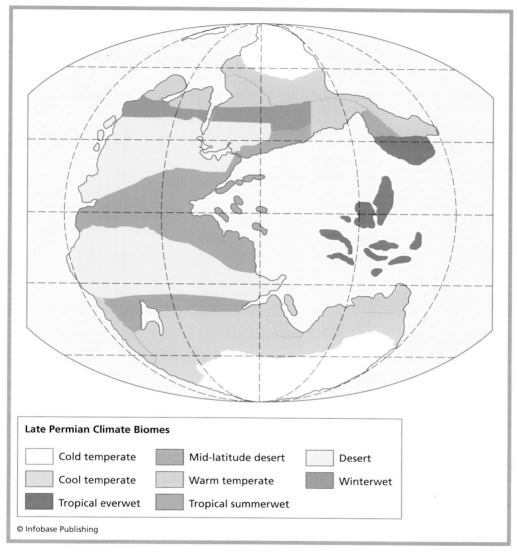

Late Permian Climate Biomes

Cold temperate	Mid-latitude desert	Desert
Cool temperate	Warm temperate	Winterwet
Tropical everwet	Tropical summerwet	

© Infobase Publishing

By the end of the Paleozoic Era, Pangaea had formed several discrete terrestrial climate zones, providing more and varied habitats for the expansion of land animals.

America and Africa were dry. Coal forests that now are located in Nova Scotia were forming in the Southern Hemisphere, near what today is East Africa. Asia existed as a series of micro-continents, not yet assembled.

By the last period of the Paleozoic Era—the Permian—the land-masses of the Northern and Southern Hemispheres had collided to form a supercontinent known as *Pangaea*. Pangaea became the single landmass from which all the continents known today would diverge. Surrounding this supercontinent was a single, vast ocean called *Panthalassa*.

Pangaea stretched from pole to pole and, because of its large mass, began to form several distinct climate zones. Some of the world became more hot and dry than it ever had been before. Seasons became more sharply defined. Ice covered the poles. The Permian Period was a time of widespread mountain forming around the world, including the ancestral Rocky Mountains in North America. Deserts covered western Pangaea. Sea levels that were relatively high in the Middle Carboniferous Period began to fluctuate regularly during the Late Carboniferous and Early Permian. Following the end-Permian mass extinction event, and crossing over into the Mesozoic Era, the world of the Early Triassic Epoch was relatively drier and hotter. These factors dramatically modified habitats and the direction of evolution for the world's plants and animals.

Formation of Soil and Ground Cover

An important early stage in the development of a habitable terrestrial environment was the formation of a viable ground cover of soil. Soil is composed of two kinds of materials. The first kind comes from rocks. When rocks are broken up by geological processes such as erosion and weathering, they can form soil particles. Mineral elements and compounds that include silicon, aluminum, iron, oxygen, calcium, magnesium, sodium, and potassium can all be found in varying amounts in soil composed of rock fragments. The other materials in soil are organic. The organic components of soil include the remains of animals and plants that have been broken down by microorganisms that live in the soil.

The first soils formed during the Ordovician Period. These soils only sparsely covered the mostly barren rock surfaces or sandy deposits of dry land. Early soils were largely mineral-based because they were almost entirely composed of weathered rocks. By the middle of the Ordovician, however, algal films had begun to reach onto the land from the oceans. Soils were probably thin but held in place by matlike, complex communities of fungi, algae, and bacteria known as **microbiotic crusts**. Examples of microbiotic-crust soils can be found today in arid regions of the world. These soils are composed of a filamentous structure that traps small particles of sand and silt to form a soil surface. Microbiotic-crust communities may have been the first inhabitants of land.

Trace evidence of microbiotic crusts goes back to Precambrian times. The development of a true soil, or humus, to underlie this crust required many more millions of years. Nutrient-rich humus consists of a mixture of minerals and organic compounds left by dead and decaying organisms. Burrowing creatures such as earthworms, ants, centipedes, and millipedes are instrumental in mixing these elements to create a rich substrate capable of encouraging the spread of plant life. The first evidence of burrowing creatures in the terrestrial fossil record occurs in the Late Ordovician Epoch. The fossil evidence suggests that ancestral centipedes and millipedes may have made these early burrows. Fossil spores found in terrestrial rocks dating from the end of the Ordovician Period indicate that by that time, the first plants had successfully begun to take root on land.

Water for Life

Water is essential for life on land. Water works in concert with ground cover to maintain a stable, self-sustaining foundation for the terrestrial ecosystem. Water is absorbed and held by soil. That soil in turn gives root to plants that bind the soil together and prevent it from being washed away by wind and rain. With the coming of the warmer climates of the Silurian Period, Earth regained its temperate and tropical zones. This encouraged the growth and spread of ground cover and soils. Rainfall nourished newly formed soils and spurred the rapid radiation of plants during the Silurian Period.

Atmospheric Carbon Dioxide and Oxygen

Life on land requires oxygen and carbon dioxide. Nearly all types of organisms use oxygen to obtain energy from organic compounds. Oxygen is an essential fuel for body tissues. Plants need carbon dioxide (CO_2) for **photosynthesis**. Carbon dioxide comes from animals when they exhale and from decaying organic matter, and is absorbed by water from the atmosphere. This exchange between living organisms and the environment is a critical factor that affects the development of all life.

The explosion of life in the sea and the rise of marine and land vertebrates happened at the same time that oxygen was becoming increasingly abundant, during Precambrian times and the Paleozoic Era. The first photosynthesizing creatures were cyanobacteria that originated about 3.5 billion years ago. The oxygenation of the oceans by the Early Paleozoic led to the rapid development of multicelled organisms. Oxygen levels in the atmosphere rose accordingly, fed by an increasing abundance of plants on both land and sea by the middle of the Paleozoic. An enormous greening of the land took place during the Carboniferous Period, as vast tropical rain forests spread throughout the hot zones of Earth's equatorial regions. Today these regions are located in North America, Europe, and Asia, and they still contain vast coal reserves—the fossilized remains of plants and animals from the Paleozoic. These same reserves helped fuel humankind's great Industrial Revolution.

During the Middle Paleozoic, through the end of the Devonian Period, levels of atmospheric carbon dioxide were much higher than levels of atmospheric oxygen—the reverse of conditions seen today. Levels of atmospheric oxygen rose steadily during the Paleozoic; this rise, coupled with a tenfold decrease in the level of CO_2, created a more inviting atmosphere for terrestrial animal life. Today, oxygen makes up about 21 percent of the atmosphere. During the Late Carboniferous Period, atmospheric oxygen levels peaked at

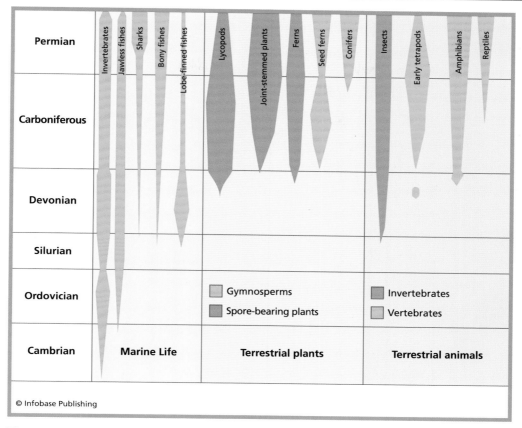

The evolution of marine and terrestrial life during the Paleozoic Era

an astounding 35 percent—a phenomenon that resulted in some spectacularly large organisms, including gigantic insects and other **arthropods**.

Ozone Protection

The Earth has a layer of **ozone** in the upper part of the oxygen-filled lower atmosphere. Ozone is made by a reaction that takes place when ultraviolet (UV) radiation from the Sun strikes oxygen molecules. When sunlight strikes oxygen molecules, the molecules are split apart; they recombine with other elements in the atmosphere to form the band of ozone that surrounds the planet. That ozone is

Earth's Changing Environment

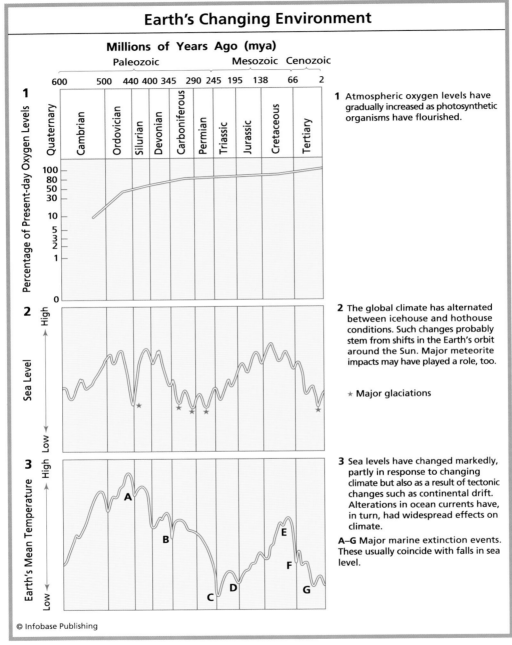

Millions of Years Ago (mya)

Paleozoic · Mesozoic · Cenozoic

1 Atmospheric oxygen levels have gradually increased as photosynthetic organisms have flourished.

2 The global climate has alternated between icehouse and hothouse conditions. Such changes probably stem from shifts in the Earth's orbit around the Sun. Major meteorite impacts may have played a role, too.

★ Major glaciations

3 Sea levels have changed markedly, partly in response to changing climate but also as a result of tectonic changes such as continental drift. Alterations in ocean currents have, in turn, had widespread effects on climate.

A–G Major marine extinction events. These usually coincide with falls in sea level.

© Infobase Publishing

Environmental conditions on Earth change at time scales ranging from decades to eons. Some changes (1) are unidirectional, but most physical and chemical changes oscillate in an irregular fashion (2–3) in response to variables such as levels of volcanism, the drift of the continents, changes in Earth's orbit, and meteorite impacts.

unstable and soon breaks apart, but it is continually replenished at the same time as it is breaking up.

Ozone is a natural filter; it prevents most of the deadly ultraviolet radiation from the Sun from striking the surface of the Earth. Without the ozone layer to shield plants and animals from UV radiation, Earth would be uninhabitable. Atmospheric oxygen levels of the early Paleozoic reached concentrations great enough to form a respectable ozone layer, thus supporting life in the seas and also on the land, where plants and animals were greatly more exposed to direct sunlight.

REQUIREMENTS FOR LIVING ON LAND

With the greening of the Middle Paleozoic world, the stage was set for the slow movement of some lines of sea organisms onto the land. For life to flourish on land, however, the land-invading organisms had to evolve certain adaptations to make life outside the water practical. Water is in many ways an ideal medium in which to live. The fluid nature of water, particularly seawater, relieves an organism from having to support its full weight. Swimming requires less energy than locomotion on land. Water carries life-giving nutrients, gases, and food particles. The ocean is also less prone to dramatic temperature changes and so provides a protective shield against temporary climate extremes in the outside air. Significant, too, is the role of water in the sexual reproduction of marine organisms. Water enables sexual reproduction to occur reliably by serving as a medium for the dispersal of reproductive molecules.

Compared with life in the water, life on land would appear to be enormously challenging. First, there is gravity to contend with. On land, an organism requires a stronger and more supportive **anatomy** to maintain its body weight and allow motion. Because they are not immersed in water, terrestrial organisms must develop ways to retain moisture and protect their bodies from drying out. Other formidable challenges to life on land include the need to develop alternative means of respiration without gills, the need to find new ways to feed, and the need to reproduce successfully outside the nurturing environment of water.

SUMMARY

This chapter explored the changing geology and climate of the Paleozoic Earth that created environments suitable for life on land.

1. Life on land was not feasible until the end of the Ordovician Period, about 444 million years ago.

2. Some of the key components that make up a successful terrestrial ecosystem are a stable ground cover of soil and plants, an abundance of water, breathable air, and shelter from ultraviolet solar radiation.

3. A craton is the large, tectonically stable interior of a continent that remains fairly intact over geologic time.

4. During the latter part of the Paleozoic Era, the topography of continental cratons became increasingly varied in terms of elevation, climate, and the availability of varied habitats.

5. An important early stage in the development of a habitable terrestrial environment was the formation of a viable ground cover of soil. The first soils were formed during the Ordovician Period and only sparsely covered the mostly barren rock surfaces of dry land.

6. Water is essential for life on land; water works in concert with ground cover to maintain a stable, self-sustaining foundation for the terrestrial ecosystem.

7. Levels of atmospheric oxygen rose steadily during the Paleozoic, creating a more inviting atmosphere for terrestrial life. During the Late Carboniferous Period, atmospheric oxygen levels peaked at an astounding 35 percent, which is 67 percent greater than the level found today.

8. Atmospheric oxygen levels of the early Paleozoic reached concentrations great enough to form a respectable ozone layer; this layer protects life in the sea and especially on land from lethal ultraviolet radiation from the Sun.

9. To live successfully on land, organisms had to evolve adaptations to cope with the greater effects of gravity and to

find new ways to breathe, to move about, to take in nourishment, to protect against changing temperatures, and to reproduce.

THE FIRST LAND PLANTS

Early Cambrian Earth encompassed two sharply different worlds. Warm, shallow oceans teemed with the many colors of life, from single-celled algae and bottom-dwelling plants to the first complex metazoans—multicelled organisms—that diversified to occupy every depth and niche of the thriving, sunlit sea. Outside of the nourishing waters of the sea, however, one-third of the planet existed as a colorless, lifeless, rocky domain. The only signs of life on dry land during the Early Cambrian Period were the dark stains left by bacteria and other single-celled organisms washed ashore by the tides and left behind by the receding waters to dry up on the oceans' barren, rocky coasts. The world beyond the coasts was devoid of green. The landscape consisted of one craggy horizon after another, the view never broken by a scrub of ground-covering plants or a patch of trees. No plants existed outside of the water. During the earliest Paleozoic, dry land was a world of unsheltered grayness.

Yet life insisted on migrating to land even though the odds were stacked strikingly against it. While the ocean contained a complete and robust ecosystem, the land had no such habitat in which to sustain life. The biological modifications needed to adapt a waterborne **physiology** to that required to thrive on dry land were enormous. This chapter traces the development of the first terrestrial plants and animals prior to the move of vertebrates from sea to land. It was a time when the world began to become green and when arthropods were the dominant creatures of the continental coasts and were expanding inland, to the interiors of the continents.

THE EVOLUTION OF EARLY LAND PLANTS

The first organisms to conquer the land were the green algal ancestors of plants. After being water bound for 500 million years, photosynthetic algae slowly crept onto near-shore rocky surfaces, where they began to adapt anatomical strategies for improving their chances of living outside the ocean. The result was myriad evolutionary changes that led to the domination of plants in all known land environments. Today, there are about 300,000 species of land plants found in terrestrial habitats.

The early evolution of plants is one of the most important in the history of life. From humble, single-celled, water-bound beginnings, plants came ashore and transformed dry land in ways that would dramatically influence the evolution of all other organisms and the ecology of the planet.

Major Plant Groups

Plants are multicellular, photosynthesizing members of the **Eukarya**—the domain of organisms with a **eukaryote** cell type that also includes animals and fungi. Most plants are green, although a select few **genera** have lost their green pigment during the course of their evolution.

During photosynthesis, the green pigment chlorophyll that is found in plant cells uses energy from sunlight to transform carbon dioxide and water into organic compounds, including free oxygen. Land plants are most responsible for altering the face of the Earth into a habitable environment for other organisms. Through the process of converting solar energy, carbon dioxide, and water into other organic compounds, plants are in actuality the key source of stored energy used by humans in such forms as coal and oil.

Most plants are land bound, although some spend a portion of their life in the water. Blue-green algae (cyanobacteria) as well as familiar seaweeds—red and brown algae—are classified as protists rather than plants. This classification is based primarily on the

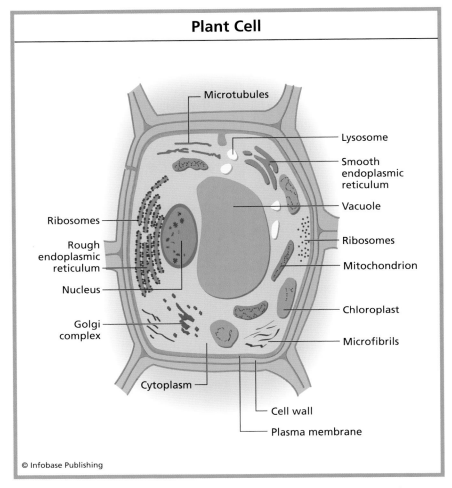

Plant Cell

Microtubules

Lysosome

Smooth endoplasmic reticulum

Vacuole

Ribosomes

Ribosomes

Rough endoplasmic reticulum

Mitochondrion

Nucleus

Golgi complex

Chloroplast

Microfibrils

Cytoplasm

Cell wall

Plasma membrane

© Infobase Publishing

The eukaryote cell of a plant, one function of which is photosynthesis.

composition of these organisms' genetic relationships. Green algae are genetically linked to the earliest land plants and can arguably be classified as either plants or protists.

Land plants exist in many varieties but are united by several common characteristics. The most fundamental defining trait of plants is the way they handle water and nutrients to nourish themselves. **Vascular plants** have **conducting systems** inside their

Nonvascular plants include mosses and hornworts.

stems and leaves to transport water and food. **Nonvascular plants** lack vascular tissue and a conducting system; instead, they absorb water and nutrients through a sparse layer of specialized absorbent cells.

These two large categories of land plants can be divided further into four major groups:

- *Nonvascular plants*, including mosses, liverworts, and hornworts. These plants are found in damp, shady places and cannot survive for long in areas that dry out for long periods. The water-absorbing cells of these plants can be highly efficient. Sphagnum peat moss can absorb up to 25 times its weight in water. There are about 16,600 living species of nonvascular plants. Nonvascular plants were the first land plants and rose during the first half of the Paleozoic Era. The earliest widespread land plants were probably of this variety.
- *Seedless vascular plants,* including club mosses, ferns, whisk ferns, and horsetails. There are about 12,400 living species of **seedless vascular plants**. Seedless vascular plants rose to dominate the second half of the Paleozoic Era.

Seedless vascular plants include ferns and horsetails.

- *Gymnosperms.* These are seed plants with a protective cone or other body for their seed embryos. **Gymnosperms** do not produce fruits or flowers. Conifers (evergreen trees), seed ferns, and cycads are found in this group. There are about 600 known living species of gymnosperms. Gymnosperms first appeared in the latter Paleozoic Era but became dominant during the Mesozoic Era.
- *Angiosperms,* the flowering plants. The **angiosperms** were the last of the great plant lineages to evolve; but today, they dominate the Earth, with more than 250,000 known living species. These plants utilize flowers to attract pollinators and also encase their seeds in fruits that, when separated from the plant, can aid in the dispersal of seeds. Angiosperms rose during the Late Mesozoic and became the dominant form of land plant during the Cenozoic Era.

Plant Adaptations for Living on Land

Plants were pioneers—the first organisms to colonize dry land. Adapting for life on land required several key modifications.

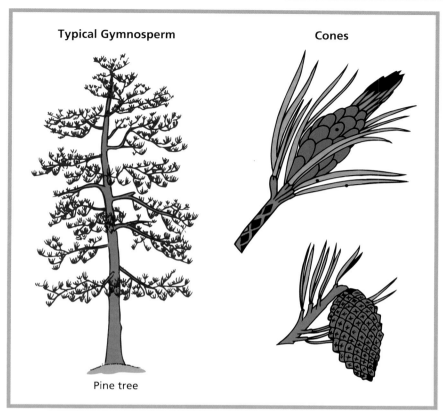

Typical Gymnosperm

Cones

Pine tree

Gymnosperms are seed plants with a protected cone or other body for their seed embryos, such as conifers (evergreen trees), seed ferns, and cycads.

Plants originated in the nourishing environment of the water. Life on land required plants to develop a way to reduce water loss and the drying effects of **desiccation**. This protection came in the form of a waxy outer covering called a **cuticle**. The cuticle is a thin, impermeable covering that grows on the outside surface of the exposed parts of a plant. In addition to slowing water loss, the cuticle may sometimes protect a plant from the harmful effects of ultraviolet solar radiation—a danger that was more acute for the first land organisms than it is for today's because in the Early Paleozoic Era, Earth's atmosphere was still developing its protective ozone shield.

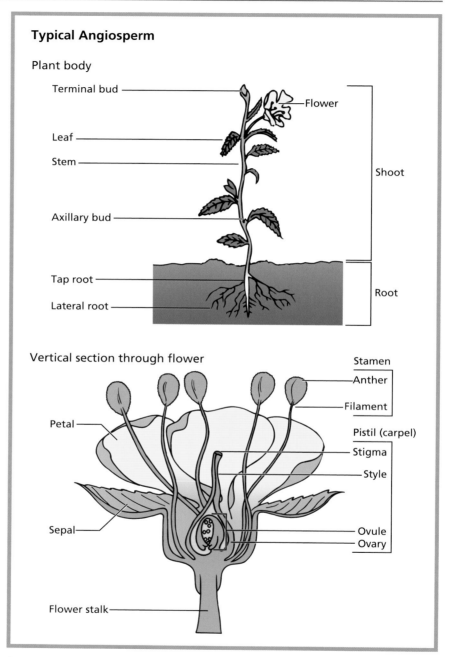

Typical Angiosperm

Plant body

Terminal bud

Flower

Leaf

Stem

Shoot

Axillary bud

Tap root

Root

Lateral root

Vertical section through flower

Stamen

Anther

Filament

Petal

Pistil (carpel)

Stigma

Style

Sepal

Ovule

Ovary

Flower stalk

Angiosperms, the flowering plants, utilize flowers to attract pollinators, and some encase their seeds in fruits to aid in their dispersal.

Plants need to breathe; this, too, posed a challenge for the first inhabitants of the land. Now that they no longer were immersed in water, plants on land needed to develop a new physiological technique: a way to grab carbon dioxide molecules from the air. Plants evolved a network of tiny pores on their outer surfaces for this purpose. Called **stomata**, these pores enable an exchange of gases between the plant and the outside air, making photosynthesis possible.

Plants living in the water are held up or suspended by the buoyancy of the marine environment. On land, larger plants must lift themselves from the ground so that they do not collapse under their own weight. This is accomplished by a skeletonlike structure of stems, branches, and trunks that gives strength and shape to land plants. Early land plants evolved such structures and, as a result, expanded their habitable environment in a vertical direction. This dramatically—and literally—increased the range of terrestrial plants over and above the flat surface of the ground, making possible taller plants including trees.

The vascular systems of land plants were another key evolutionary innovation that enabled such plants to thrive. These systems improved the plants' ability to conduct water and nourishing minerals to different parts of their structures. Roots evolved as a specialized means to absorb water. These increasingly effective methods of providing food and energy led to the growth and diversity of all kinds of plants.

One final challenge for plants living on land was to find a means to reproduce effectively. In the marine environment, plants passed sperm to egg through the medium of water. Plants in a terrestrial habitat evolved many different solutions to the challenge of achieving the union of sperm and egg. Most of these solutions depend on reproductive cells called spores. Spores can be blown through the air, transported by available surface water, and transported by pollinating insects to make plant reproduction possible.

Many of these plant adaptations were mirrored by the evolution of invertebrate and vertebrate animals for life on the land. Plants

Photosynthesis

Water + light = chemical energy

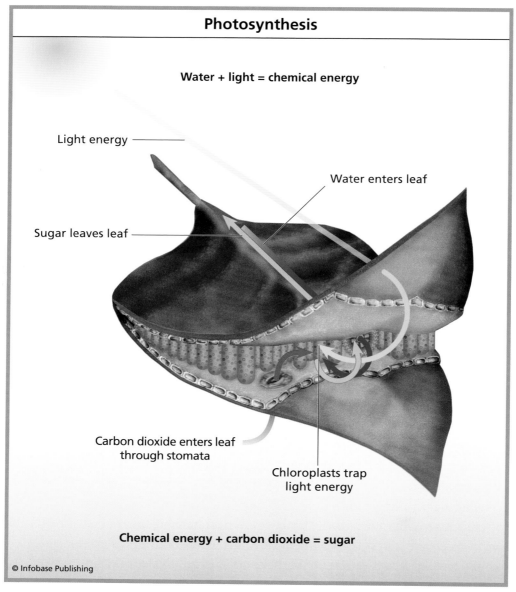

Light energy

Water enters leaf

Sugar leaves leaf

Carbon dioxide enters leaf
through stomata

Chloroplasts trap
light energy

Chemical energy + carbon dioxide = sugar

© Infobase Publishing

Plants nourish themselves through photosynthesis. Using a network of tiny pores, or stomata, on their outer surface enables plants to exchange gases with the outside air, allowing them to breathe.

share with some animal groups the internalization of vital body systems such as sexual organs, the development of a protective outer skin, and functions such as gas exchange.

The Origin and Evolution of Land Plants

Photosynthesizing algae first arose in the oceans. As improbable as it may seem, a single species of green algae, living in the water, was likely responsible for giving rise to every form of land plant that followed. This was a monumental step in the evolution of life on Earth, yet it was also a kind of accident—an accident repeated over and over until life stuck to dry land once and for all. It began when near-coastal colonies of algae mats—stromatolites—became exposed to the air when the tides waned. The slow adaptation of green algae to dry land was pushed further along by the action of waves that left bits of algae stranded on exposed dry surfaces on the shore. Over time, through the process of **natural selection**, some of these algae became hearty enough to exist and reproduce outside of the water as a biotic smear on an exposed rock surface.

Lichens were one of the earliest land organisms to prosper. Not classified as plants, lichens are a form of fungi that live in symbiosis with photosynthetic algae or cyanobacteria. Even today, lichens can be found in some of Earth's harshest environments. Lichens were probably capable of surviving the extreme conditions of the Early Paleozoic Earth, where harsh changes in temperature and long periods of drought were common. Fossil evidence shows that lichens were probably widespread by the Early Devonian Epoch, and some scientists place the origin of lichens to the very beginning of the Cambrian Period.

By the Late Cambrian Period, oxygen had probably risen to levels adequate to sustain a viable ozone layer in the atmosphere—an essential shield to protect organisms directly exposed to lethal ultraviolet radiation from the Sun. The next requirement for sustaining life on land was the development of a ground-covering soil. Although fossil evidence of microbiotic crusts or mats dating from the Precambrian suggests that near-shore soils were beginning to take shape even in the Early Cambrian, the appearance of true soils underlying these crustal mats was slow in coming. It took 100 million years or more for the thin bacterial and fungal carpets of the Early Cambrian to thicken into soil covers capable of supporting the first traces of plants and small animals such as arthropods and ancestral worms. Spore traces of early plants show that by the Late Ordovician Epoch, the terrestrial ecosystem had become fixed and stable enough to support the relatively sudden and explosive expansion of land plants during the Silurian and Devonian Periods.

Early Nonvascular Plants

Fossil evidence of ground cover other than lichens is found in deposits from the Middle Ordovician Epoch and consists of isolated spores that resemble those of modern liverworts. These spores have what is called a tetrad design and consist of a four-part membrane with a decay-resistant wall for housing the spores. One might say that these liverwort-type spores came in four-packs. Liverworts are good candidates for one of the earliest land plants because they can been seen today living symbiotically with algae, sometimes on microbiotic crusts that are thought to be similar to the earliest kinds of soils.

Mosses and hornworts make up two other families of likely early nonvascular plants. Like liverworts, mosses and hornworts do not have roots, and most varieties reproduced by dispersing spores. Mosses can resemble liverworts but sometimes have twisting branches with leaflike structures, though these are all nonvascular features. Mosses commonly hug the surface to which they are attached and can be found thriving in moist environments.

Hornworts also grow in damp, humid places. They have large, horn-shaped leaves clustered around the flattened body of the plant. Like mosses, some varieties of living hornworts are commonly found growing on the bark of trees.

Seedless Vascular Plants

Fossil spores from the Early Silurian Period to the Middle Devonian Epoch show a decline in the diversity of tetrad-type spores in favor of simpler, single plant spores that were dispersed individually. Although evidence associating these single spores with specific kinds of plants is rare in the fossil record from that time, spores such as this are used by seedless vascular plants and by some **extant** species of nonvascular plants such as mosses and hornworts. The protective outer walls of these single spores were improved over the protective sheathes of the tetrad spores of nonvascular plants; this improvement made the single spores more likely to spread and prosper than their predecessors. This is exactly what happened. As seedless nonvascular plants arose, they swarmed into niches once occupied by nonvascular plants. This effectively restricted the liverworts, mosses, and hornworts to the habitats they now hold.

Thus began an extraordinary second phase in the evolution of land plants. Between 480 million and 360 million years ago (Middle Ordovician Epoch to the Early Carboniferous Period), land plants made a transition from their humble beginnings as mere rock-covering smears and low-lying ground cover. They developed a variety of new anatomical structures, reproductive schemes for the survival of their species, and adaptations for many varied habitats. It was a green revolution on land that transformed rocky, barren continents into life-supporting terrestrial habitats.

The first definitive fossils of land plants come from Middle Silurian deposits of Northern Europe and Late Silurian deposits of Australia, Bolivia, and northwestern China. These fossils include specimens of seedless vascular plants, such as *Rhynia* and *Cooksonia*, with internal channels for conducting water and nutrients. Club mosses such as *Baragwanathia* also are found from this time, as are several plants such as *Salopella* whose connection to modern families of plants is not yet understood.

The earliest vascular land plants were **morphologically** simple and small. None had roots; they existed as creeping plants that spread across the ground. *Cooksonia*—found in Middle Silurian deposits of central Asia, Europe, eastern North America, and Brazil—consisted of upright stalks only about one inch (2.5 cm) tall. *Steganotheca* (Late Silurian, Great Britain) was a little more bushlike and stood two inches (5 cm) tall.

Going into the Devonian Period, there was a sharp difference in plant biology. The short, barely rooted, and flimsy experiments in vascularity of the Silurian gave way to stronger, more robust

Ferns are seedless, vascular, spore-bearing ground cover. They are noted for their creeping stems, photosynthetic featherlike leaves or fronds, and fibrous roots similar to those of seed plants.

vascular plants. The stalks of these plants were woodier; this allowed them to grow taller and distribute their spores more widely. By the Middle Devonian Epoch, the rise of vascular plants was leading to great diversity in plant design and size. *Psilophyton* was an early vascular plant reinforced by robust bundles of conducting channels. Some specimens measure more than three feet (1 m) tall. Many times taller than *Cooksonia* and *Steganotheca*, *Psilophyton* was a stepping-stone to the largest and most successful seedless vascular plants—the **lycopods**, ferns, and sphenopsids (horsetails).

One of the most spectacular groups of early seedless vascular plants were the lycopods. The lycopods were the first major group of vascular plants; they arose during the Silurian Period and became widespread on a worldwide basis by the Carboniferous. The evolutionary origins of the lycopods are unclear, but they may be related to the earlier *Cooksonia*. Lycopods developed strong root structures and hard stalks to resist desiccation in hot, tropical climates. The largest members of this group grew to be an astounding 100 feet (30 m) tall and formed huge forests. Unlike in modern trees, the leaves of lycopods were attached directly to the stalk of the main trunk. As a lycopod grew taller, it shed its leaves, leaving only a cluster of leaves at the top. This gave the tree a distinctive, umbrellalike appearance. As the leaves were shed, they left a diamond-shaped pattern of scars on the trunk, a visually distinctive feature for which these fossils are known. The spores of lycopods were borne on fertile leaves. Modern remnants of lycopods are not nearly as spectacular as their ancestors; they include the branching club mosses and "ground pine."

Ferns arose during the latter part of the Devonian as seedless, spore-bearing ground cover. By the Carboniferous Period, many fern varieties had become widespread, and some species towered over the coal forest as large trees. There currently are more than 10,000 species of true ferns that trace their lineage back to the Paleozoic; this makes ferns the most prevalent type of modern seedless vascular plant. Ferns are noted for their creeping stems; their photosynthetic featherlike leaves or fronds; and their fibrous roots, similar to those of seed plants. Ferns were one of the first groups of plants with significant root structures. These structures further strengthened the plants' physical stature, improved their intake of nutrients from the soil, and encouraged ferns to grow larger and taller. Fern spores are found as small dots on the underside of the leaves.

Sphenopsids were seedless vascular plants that evolved during the Devonian Period, at about the same time as ferns. The name sphenopsid means "joint-stemmed"; the plants owe their name to the structure of their long, hollow, jointed stems. The only modern-day representatives of the sphenopsids are 15 species of the horsetail.

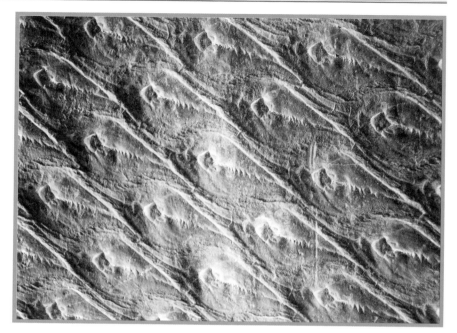

This image shows Lepidodendron, an extinct lycopod (or giant club moss), which is a spectacular early seedless vascular plant.

The living sphenopsids include perennial species that are most at home when rooted in sandy soil along a riverbank or stream. Leaves of modern varieties may be broomlike or may resemble a horse's tail, with the thin, needlelike leaves attached at the jointed points in the hollow stalk. The spores of sphenopsids cluster with the leaves. One variety of living sphenopsid—the scouring rush—has a fibrous texture that made it a popular tool in the early American kitchen for scouring pots and pans. The heyday of the sphenopsids spanned the Carboniferous and Permian Periods, when some varieties towered as tall as 100 feet (30 m). The extinct genus *Calamites* had a bamboolike stalk with vertical ribbing and needlelike leaves. *Calamites* grew to more than 31 feet (9.5 m) tall, and its fossils are often found in deposits of Carboniferous Period coal-bearing formations.

(continues on page 50)

THINK ABOUT IT

The Early Evolution of Leaves

Leaves are the primary factories of photosynthesis in vascular plants. Photosynthesis occurs when light energy from the Sun, carbon dioxide in the air, and water are chemically combined to create food energy for the plant inside the leaves. As a byproduct of this process, leaves release oxygen into the air and enable plants to maintain an atmospheric balance of carbon dioxide and oxygen that sustains the life of invertebrate and vertebrate animals.

The size, shape, and arrangement of leaves are important to their function and affect the amount of sunlight that the plant can absorb to fuel photosynthesis. The earliest vascular plants did not have leaves as are commonly seen today. Several environmental factors, including changes in the makeup of Earth's atmosphere, influenced the evolution of the first leaves.

The first vascular plants that colonized the land during the Middle Silurian Period were leafless. They absorbed sunlight and carried out photosynthesis through their stems. Early vascular plants such as the extinct *Cooksonia* and other related rhyniophids consisted only of branching stems that grew low to the ground. Fossil evidence of the first leaves does not appear in the fossil record until about 40 million years later, near the end of the Devonian Period.

The appearance of plants with leaves was a monumental event in the natural history of the Earth. Plants with leaves form the foundation of a worldwide ecosystem that to this day is vital to the survival of all other animals. Why it took so long for leaves to evolve from the first vascular plants has been a source of puzzlement to plant **paleontologists**. After all, leaves greatly improve the ability of plants to photosynthesize, furthering their survival and distribution.

In 2001, a team of British paleobotanists that included David J. Beerling, Colin P. Osborne, and William G. Chaloner tackled the mystery of the

(continues)

(continued)

slow emergence of the first leaves. The team noted a correlation between a tenfold drop in the concentration of carbon dioxide in the atmosphere, the rise of atmospheric oxygen, and the appearance and diversification of plant leaves. This change in the composition of the atmosphere occurred between 410 million and 370 million years ago, during the Devonian Period, and corresponds well with the appearance and design of leaves. For proof of the concept, the scientific team turned to the fossil record, where they focused on finding fossil evidence. What they found dramatically illustrated their point. As the world became more habitable for oxygen-breathing organisms, so, too, did the size, shape, and effectiveness of leaf blades improve. From the simple branching stems of *Rhynia*, early leaf structures emerged in the form of stem branches in *Psilophyton*; in the form of side branches in *Actinoxylon,* to further improve the number of photosynthesizing elements; and in the development of fuller leaves with infilling of spaces between the branching stems, as in *Archaeopteris.*

(continued from page 48)

The boom in seedless vascular plants during the Devonian led to the spectacular spread of vast tropical swamps and forests. Spore-bearing ferns and seed ferns formed a dense layer of mid-height vegetation under a canopy of lycopsids, sphenopsids, and the towering progymnosperm, *Archaeoptreris*. Growing big and tall was the rule of the day as branching plants of all types competed for exposure to sunlight.

The seedless vascular plants dominated the Paleozoic terrestrial ecosystem; however, as the world of the Permian Period began to cool and dry out, land plants began another important transition in their evolution. In the shadow of the seedless vascular plants were the first seeded plants, or gymnosperms, that would come to dominate the next important phase of plant evolution.

Early Gymnosperms

Gymnosperms—the "naked seed" plants—were the focus of the next great evolutionary triumph for land vegetation. Seed plants did not dominate terrestrial environments until the Mesozoic Era, but their appearance during the Late Paleozoic in the form of seed ferns, towering trees such as *Cordaites*, and shrublike plants such as *Glossopteris* was an auspicious marker between the old tropical world of the Paleozoic and the drier, more temperate habitats of the Mesozoic.

Seedless plants thrived in the swamps and forests of the Middle Paleozoic because they required moisture to reproduce. Liquid water was needed for the sperm and egg components of these spore-bearing plants to join and fertilize. Early seedless plants were at first restricted to ground-hugging forms that lived near bodies of water. As the world became hotter and wetter, and vascular plants grew taller, they extended their range to the humid interiors of expansive tropical forests. In the Devonian and Carboniferous Periods, the water that was needed to spread and fertilize spores came in the form of rain and humidity that frequently drenched the leaves of plants living in the densely vegetative habitats.

The early gymnosperms adapted to cooler, drier, and more elevated environments by developing a way to protect their seeds from desiccation. Spore-bearing plants before them produced tiny plants called gametophytes that contained both eggs and sperm. Water was needed to join these reproductive cells together so that fertilization could take place. The tiny, unprotected gametophytes were highly susceptible to drying out and would not survive outside of the moist environment of the swamp. Gametophytes also were not very mobile; new plants grew close to the parent plant. This hindered the ability of a plant to distribute its offspring over a wider geographic area.

Gymnosperms found a way to protect their reproductive cells from desiccation. Each plant produced male and female cones.

Telangium, an extinct gymnosperm from the Carboniferous Period

The male cones produced pollen grains, and the female cones produced the beginnings of a true seed. The wind carried the male pollen to the seed-bearing female cone, and in that cone the pollen fertilized the egg. The fertilized egg then grew within the protective shell of the seed covering, where it fed on nutrients found within the seed itself. Not only did this advance protect the seed from drying out, it also provided a mobile seed that could be spread by the wind, further extending the range of such plants.

Seed plants first appeared in the Carboniferous Period and were probably related to a group of seedless vascular plants known as **progymnosperms**. *Archaeopteris* is one such ancestor whose fossils are found in Late Devonian forests around the world. Carboniferous Period *Archaeopteris* reproduced by spores like a seedless fern, but it had a woody bark—a protective covering like that found in a typical conifer from the Mesozoic. As such, *Archaeopteris* represents an intermediate stage in the adaptation of plants from the moist, humid habitats of the Middle Paleozoic to the drier, cooler environments leading into the Mesozoic.

Significant climate shifts during the Permian Period dried the once fertile coal swamps and encouraged the spread of hearty gymnosperms. With the gymnosperms came a great expansion of terrestrial habitats into higher elevations and floodplains. Although the most diverse period of gymnosperm evolution was still ahead, several varieties of these seed-bearing plants became plentiful during the Late Paleozoic Era.

Seed ferns were the earliest gymnosperms. Their leaves resembled seedless ferns, but these plants reproduced by way of seeds. *Elkinsia*, from the Late Devonian Epoch, is the earliest of these seed ferns. The first seed ferns did not have cones but produced seeds along their branches in protective, cuplike capsules.

Cordaites, which are now extinct, were some of the tallest common gymnosperms of the Late Paleozoic. Growing up to 100 feet (30 m), *Cordaites* had tall, branchless trunks with a tuft of long, strap-shaped leaves bunched at the top. Seed-bearing cones were clustered among the leaves. Found primarily in North America and Europe, the *Cordaites* disappeared at the end of the Permian Period.

Glossopteris is another notable gymnosperm from the end of the Paleozoic. Found in terrestrial environments from the southern

The first seed ferns, such as *Elkinsia*, did not have cones but produced seeds along their branches in protective cuplike capsules.

Paleozoic supercontinent of Gondwana—India, Australia, Africa, South America, and Antarctica—*Glossopteris* first appeared in the Permian Period and was extinct by the Late Triassic Epoch. The broad, flat, tongue-shaped leaves of this tree ranged from four inches (10 cm) to more than three feet (0.9 m) long and may have been shed on a seasonal basis. Male and female reproductive cells appear to have been produced on different leaves, but the way they were contained—e.g., on a pollen stalk or in a sack—has not yet been determined with certainty by examining their fossils. Although many fossil leaves of *Glossopteris* have been discovered, the same cannot be said for the trunk or body of this genus. It may have been a large shrub or small tree similar to a cycad and measuring 13 to 20 feet (4–6 m) tall.

Following closely on the migration of plants to dry land were the invertebrate organisms that provided the ancestral stock of today's land arthropods. These included insects, spiderlike creatures, mites, ancestral scorpions, worms, millipedes, centipedes, and their kin.

SUMMARY

This chapter traced the development of the first terrestrial plants and animals prior to the move of vertebrates from sea to land.

1. The first organisms to conquer the land were green algae that were the ancestors of land plants.

2. Plants are multicellular, photosynthesizing members of the Eukarya, the domain of organisms with a eukaryote cell type that also includes animals and fungi.

3. Vascular plants have conducting systems inside their stems and leaves to transport water and food. Nonvascular plants lack vascular tissue and a conducting system; they absorb water and nutrients through a sparse layer of specialized absorbent cells.

4. The four major plant groups are the nonvascular plants, including mosses, liverworts, and hornworts; the seedless vascular plants, including club mosses, ferns, whisk ferns, and horsetails; the gymnosperms, including conifers (evergreen

trees), seed ferns, and cycads; and the angiosperms, the flowering plants.

5. Plant adaptations for living on land include the development of a waxy outer covering to protect against the drying effects of desiccation; the development of tiny surface pores called stomata for gas exchange and making photosynthesis possible; and the development of a supportive, skeletonlike structure to help the plants stand up out of water.

6. Lichens—a form of fungi that live in symbiosis with photosynthetic algae—were some of the earliest land organisms.

7. Fossil evidence consisting of isolated tetrad-type spores suggests that ancestral plant species of liverworts and hornworts lived on land in the Middle Ordovician Epoch.

8. Fossils of nontetrad single plant spores from the Early Silurian Period to the Middle Devonian Epoch indicate the development of the first, basal seedless vascular plants. The first definitive fossils of seedless vascular plants come from Middle Silurian deposits of Northern Europe and latter Silurian deposits of Australia, Bolivia, and northwestern China.

9. Lycopods, ferns, and sphenopsids (horsetails) were highly successful types of seedless vascular plants that lived during the Late Paleozoic Era.

10. Seed plants—the gymnosperms—first appeared in the Carboniferous Period.

11. Gymnosperms developed seeds that were less susceptible to desiccation; this gave the gymnosperms an advantage as world climates became drier and cooler by the end of the Permian Period.

3

THE FIRST LAND ANIMALS

The first animals to exploit the new terrestrial habitat created by land plants were descendants of marine-based arthropods, the most diverse of all animal groups. Arthropods today include crustaceans (including marine-living lobsters, crabs, and shrimp); arachnids (including spiders, mites, ticks, and scorpions, all with eight legs); centipedes and millipedes (with 30 or more legs); and insects (including beetles, bees, flies, butterflies, and others, all with a three-part body, six legs, and, in most species, wings).

What made the arthropods ideally suited for the transition to land was their basic body plan. Their tough outer skin covering and thin, jointed appendages left few soft parts exposed to the evaporative effects of dry air. Legs also provided the arthropods with the means to move about on dry land—to navigate obstacles and make their way despite the greater pull of gravity that comes with living outside the water.

The initial transition of plants from water to land occurred only once, and from those earliest pioneering terrestrial adaptations sprouted all other lineages of land plants in succession. One reason for this was that plants in their present-day form—as vascular, photosynthesizing organisms—existed in the ocean only in the most primitive algal forms just before their movement to dry land. Early plants progressed through various stages of adaptation to dry land; this resulted in increased diversification over time into the four main groups of extant plants.

In contrast to plants, arthropods were already well established in oceans, lakes, and streams prior to their migration to land. Representatives of the different groups of arthropods made their transitions to land independently, and each group worked out its own unique solutions to living in a dry habitat. This transition took place over a span of about 160 million years, from the Late Ordovician to the Late Carboniferous Period. While the first transitioning arthropods preceded the first transitioning vertebrates onto land, by the Carboniferous Period, both groups were thriving in the vast, tropical swamps and forests associated with coal-age fossil deposits. The existence of millipedes, centipedes, insects, and spiders alongside the first tetrapods sustained a robust ecosystem in which most animals were predators or scavengers. The fossil record provides little evidence for the eating of living plants by either arthropods or vertebrates until the Late Carboniferous Epoch and the Permian Period. Until that time, it is presumed that arthropods either were detritus eaters—feeders on dead organic matter, such as plant remains—or predators that ate other arthropods, such as insects.

Only three of the four groups of arthropods are represented by land species during the Paleozoic. Today, the crustaceans, although mostly marine based, also have terrestrial members in the form of the Isopoda (wood lice or pill bugs) and some species of hermit crabs, but none of these were among the first line of land animals to leave the oceans during the Paleozoic.

MYRIAPODA: MILLIPEDES AND CENTIPEDES

Millipedes and centipedes are members of the group of arthropods known as Myriapoda, a name that is Greek for "many feet." All of the appendages of the Myriapoda are single-branched, or **uniramous**. Most arthropod limbs are **biramous,** or double-branched; they consist of a sturdy, weight-supporting limb that also has a branching, feathery, gill limb attached. Many kinds of arthropods have lost the gill limb, leaving only the supporting, uniramous walking limb.

The first evidence for land animals is found in the form of **trace fossils** from the Late Ordovician Epoch. This evidence, which consists of preserved burrows, suggests that millipedes had evolved by that time and had become an important part of the evolving terrestrial ecosystem. The first definitive body fossils of millipedes are found in Late Silurian and Early Devonian deposits in Scotland. The Middle to Late Devonian fossil record of the Myriapoda is scant, but centipedelike specimens have been found in fossil bearing rocks known from the Gilboa fauna in New York and other North American and European sites. Even though there is a slight gap in the fossil record, the Myriapoda continued to thrive and diversify well into the Carboniferous Period.

One long-lasting group of millipedes was the Arthropleuridae. They were geographically widespread, and their fossils have been found in rocks that range in age from the Late Silurian to Early Permian Period, in Europe and North America. Unlike the familiar millipedes whose segmented body armor is usually rounded or cylinder shaped, the arthropleurids had broad, flat backs that hid their many legs. Arthropleurid remains have been found mostly in such Northern Hemisphere locales as Scotland; Kazakhstan (an area in central Asia and easternmost Europe); Pennsylvania and New York; and Quebec, in Canada. At least one genus has been discovered in Australia.

Arthropleurids ranged in size from the few millimeters of *Microdecemplex* to the astounding *Arthropleura*, which could have been more than six feet (1.8 m) long. Trace fossils associated with *Arthropleura* were recently discovered in Late Carboniferous deposits of Kentucky and New Mexico in 2005 and 2006. The New Mexico trackway resembles two parallel tire tracks. The tracks suggest that this specimen was at least eight feet long (2.4 m)—a true monster millipede of its time, or of any time. Racing through the fern-shaded undercover of ancient swamplands, *Arthropleura* existed during a time when present-day New Mexico was closer to the equator. It was a warm, moist habitat in which *Arthropleura* may have been a deposit feeder as well as a top predator; it may have eaten decaying organic remains on the floor of the forest as well as insects and perhaps small vertebrates. *Arthropleura* is not directly related to modern millipedes; it was part of a family of gigantic species that

(continues on page 63)

THINK ABOUT IT

Atmospheric Oxygen and Gigantism in Paleozoic Arthropods

The atmosphere of Earth underwent many radical shifts in its basic chemistry during the Paleozoic Era. Most significantly for terrestrial animals, geochemical studies of sedimentary rock and oxygen molecules in the air confirm a marked increase in the amount of atmospheric oxygen during the Late Paleozoic, followed by a sharp decline. This oxygen pulse was accompanied by equally dramatic shifts in the amount of carbon dioxide in the air. Compared to present-day oxygen levels of 21 percent of the atmosphere, the concentration of free oxygen during the Late Paleozoic peaked in the Carboniferous at 35 percent and then dropped to 15 percent by the end of the Permian. Much of this expansion of atmospheric oxygen is attributed to the rise of vascular land plants whose photosynthesis produced oxygen as a byproduct.

Changes in the makeup of the atmosphere affected the evolution of the first animals. During the transition from water to land, the first terrestrial inhabitants faced challenging climate conditions, particularly with regard to the animals' ability to develop effective physiological means for extracting oxygen from the air. Water-based arthropods breathed using gills. Arthropods on land developed a variety of unique respiratory strategies. Insects evolved a particularly effective method of breathing without lungs. They bypassed their circulatory system and directly infused their tissues with oxygen through a network of tiny, branching tubes that ran from the surface of their hard, outer skin. The insect respiratory system is effective with only a meager amount of oxygen in the air—a critical requirement during the early stages of insect evolution, when there was decidedly less oxygen available. By the end of the Devonian Period and leading into the Carboniferous, however, oxygen levels on the planet rose rapidly, as terrestrial plans spread far and wide. The effect on the evolution of insects was dramatic.

The fossil record shows that the largest insects of all time lived during the Late Paleozoic, particularly in the tropical coal forests of the

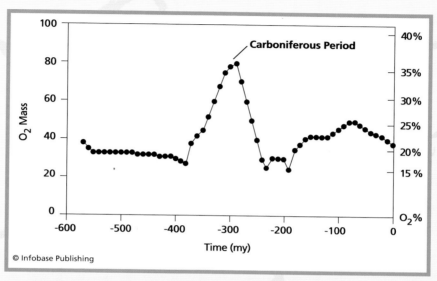

Levels of atmospheric oxygen over the past 550 million years, showing a dramatic spike during the Carboniferous Period.

Carboniferous Period. Cockroaches, dragonflies, mayflies, and other insects grew to unprecedented sizes. One traditional explanation for the evolution of larger and larger insects was the defense against predators. Most creatures of that time were active predators, and one clear defense against being eaten was for natural selection to favor those larger members of insect species that were able to survive until reproductive maturity. Another factor that contributed to gigantism in insects was the insect respiratory system. While insects can indeed survive on a small concentration of oxygen in the atmosphere, their system of diffusing oxygen directly into their tissues also allowed for spectacular growth when there was an overabundance of oxygen, as there was in the Late Paleozoic. Larger insects had more surface area with which to absorb oxygen, and these

(continues)

(continued)

larger insects evidently passed along this trait to new generations. The result, after many millions of years, was a world populated by unusually large insects, until the upper limits of size for this type of growth were met.

The concentration of atmospheric oxygen during the Late Paleozoic also had implications on the development of insect flight. Specifically, more oxygen in the air made the air denser. This made it easier for winged insects to gain lift as they took flight. Smaller wings would have been able to carry more weight. The success of the first fliers led to successive generations of specialization in wing design and efficiency. In large part, this evolutionary milestone was made possible by the dense atmosphere that encouraged the development of early flight.

If insects and other arthropods, such as scorpions and spiders, were so successful in exploiting an oxygen-rich environment, why, then, did there not evolve dragonflies as big as airplanes and scorpions the size of tanks? The answer is that there are thresholds imposed by the laws of physics that limit the body size of organisms. In the case of arthropods, the body size is limited by the very respiratory system that enabled the organism to grow so large in the first place. A diffusion type of breathing, in which oxygen is fed to the tissues by surface tubes, is extraordinarily effective in smaller animals. If an insect species grows larger, however, this form of gas exchange works against further growth. Paleontologist Richard Fortey points out that as the surface area—the outside skin of the exoskeleton—of an arthropod increases, the inner volume of the animal also increases, but by a factor of eight. There is a point at which a larger version of the same animal simply would not be able to take in enough oxygen to feed its tissues and organs.

A second physical limitation is also related to the tiny trachea, or air diffusion tubes. As the limbs of an arthropod grow larger, the inside surfaces of the air tubes become stronger and stiffer. There is a point at which the tubes become difficult to flex, and any such air passages to the tissues of an arthropod's legs would make the legs too stiff to move. Either prospect—the inability to breathe or the inability to walk—provides biological constraints for the evolution of arthropods of unlimited size.

(continued from page 59)

thrived in response to the abundance of oxygen in the Carboniferous atmosphere. When Earth's atmosphere changed in the Permian Period, and oxygen levels declined to levels that are more equivalent to today's, *Arthropleura* was among many large species of arthropods that became extinct. Whether or not a lower oxygen level was responsible for the extinction is not fully understood, although it may have been a contributing factor to the demise of such a large arthropod.

INSECTA

Insects are members of the arthropod class Insecta. They are the largest group of organisms on the planet and account for more than half of the named species known to science. Doubtless there are tens of thousands more species of insects waiting to be detected. More

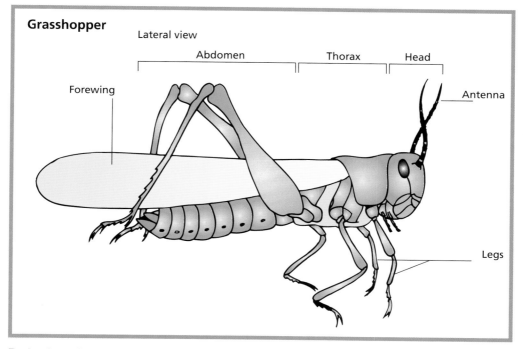

Body plan of a typical insect

MAJOR GROUPS OF INSECTA

The **taxonomy** of living insects includes 31 major groups or orders and more than 1,015 families within those groups. In addition, there are about 12 extinct groups that are known only from the fossil record. The following table includes an abridged list of the major groups of insects that account for about 75 percent of all living species. Those having roots in the Paleozoic Era are also indicated.

Group	Characteristics	Members	Appearance in Fossil Record	Approximate Number of Named Living Species
Coleoptera	Two pairs of wings with front set armored to protect the rear set of flying wings; hard exoskeleton; biting and chewing jaws	Beetles, ladybugs, click beetles	Middle Permian	360,000
Lepidoptera	Two pairs of large flying wings; hairy body; sucking mouth	Butterflies, moths	Late Cretaceous	160,000
Diptera	Two pairs of wings, with front set for flying and rear set greatly reduced; piercing and sucking mouth	House flies, mosquitoes, gnats, botflies, fruit flies	Middle Triassic	125,000
Hymenoptera	Two pairs of flying wings; advanced eyes; mobile head; some possess stingers; chewing and sucking mouth	Bees, wasps, ants	Late Triassic	130,000
Hemiptera	Two pairs of wings or wingless; piercing and sucking mouth; live on plants or suck blood	True bugs, bedbugs, leafhoppers, aphids, cicadas	Permian	85,000
Orthoptera	Two pairs of wings or wingless; biting and chewing jaws; jumpers; some of the largest insects	Grasshoppers, crickets, katydids	Late Permian	22,500
Odonata	Two pairs of flying wings; long, slender torso; chewing jaws	Dragonflies, mayflies, damselflies	Early Carboniferous	5,200
Blattaria	Two pairs of wings or wingless; biting and chewing jaws; jumpers	Cockroaches	Middle Carboniferous	4,000

Group	Characteristics	Members	Appearance in Fossil Record	Approximate Number of Named Living Species
Isoptera	Two pairs of wings but with wingless stages of development; chewing jaws; can eat wood	Termites	Late Cretaceous	2,100
Siphonaptera	Wingless; jumpers; piercing and sucking mouth; small	Fleas	Miocene	2,000
Archaeognatha and Zygentoma	Wingless; small, with three long caudal filaments; chewing jaws with external mouthparts	Bristletails, silverfish	Early Devonian	400

than 800,000 species of insects have been named. The physical traits that unite most insects include a three-part body that consists of the head, thorax, and abdomen; two pairs of wings; and three pairs of legs attached to the thorax. The head usually has one pair of uniramous (single-branched) antennae and three pairs of mouthparts that differ considerably with the type of insect. Some insects have jaws adapted for biting and chewing plants; others are equipped for piercing and sucking fluids from plants or animals.

The Early Devonian fossil deposits of Scotland known as the Rhynie Chert offer a unique window onto the world of early arthropods. It is in these deposits that many examples of the earliest known land plants and arthropods are found. The Rhynie Chert is especially important to the fossil record of insects because it is here that the earliest known forms are found. The first and best understood genus is *Rhyniella,* which was first named in 1926 based on fragmentary fossils of the insect's head. In subsequent years, other parts of this insect have been discovered, including legs, the thorax, and an abdomen discovered in 2004. *Rhyniella* was a small, wingless insect; it is believed to be related to modern springtails. Springtails are tiny, measuring only several millimeters long, and, like silverfish, are among the most basal of insects.

Rhyniella may represent an important stage in the evolution of insects, the origins of which are little understood. Recent analysis of the genetic makeup—the **genes**—of these insects suggests that they represent an evolutionary stage that branched off from the crustaceans and led to modern winged insects. Some scientists do not actually classify springtails as insects. This is because springtails appear to represent an evolutionary line related to crustaceans that may be unconnected to true insects, despite such similarities as the springtails' six-legged anatomy.

If, as some scientists believe, springtails are not true insects, then another tiny fossil specimen discovered at the same time as the original *Rhyniella* specimen may hold the key to the origin of true insects. *Rhyniognatha* consists only of a pair of well-preserved mouthparts, called mandibles, that measure only nine-tenths of a millimeter long and that can be viewed only with a powerful microscope. At the time of their discovery in 1926, the mandibles were assigned to the new genus *Rhyniognatha* and called "insectlike," but no attempt was made to place them into any clearly defined insect group. Thus did *Rhyniognatha* disappear into obscurity, like so many extra bits of scrap shale tossed aside for later investigation. In subsequent years, other claims to the earliest known true insects were made from slightly younger fossil deposits, most notably some possible body fragments of a wingless insect from Late Devonian deposits in Gilboa, New York. In 2004, however, Michael Engel, an entomologist from the University of Kansas, and David Grimaldi, a zoologist from the American Museum of Natural History, revealed the results of a closer examination of the long-ignored *Rhyniognatha* specimen. What they determined is that *Rhyniognatha* has traits ascribable to winged insects even though no fossilized wings or related body parts were discovered. *Rhyniognatha*'s mouthparts are consistent with the chewing lifestyle associated with winged insects. This discovery suggests that the development of wings occurred long before what is currently known from the first definitive fossils of winged insects from the Late Carboniferous Period.

After the Middle Devonian, the fossil record for insects goes nearly dark during the Late Devonian Epoch and Early Carboniferous Period. This is due to a lack of known terrestrial fossil deposits of the appropriate age and habitat. The abundance of fossils documenting the Late Carboniferous Period reveals a world full of many varieties and sizes of insects, however. Winged insects, cockroaches, mayflies, and true bugs took hold during the Late Paleozoic, giving root to many modern families of insects. A guide to the most prominent groups of Paleozoic insects follows.

Archaeognatha and Zygentoma: Basal, Wingless Insects

The wingless bristletails, or archaeognathans, represent an ancient evolutionary stage that links the wingless and winged insects. The extinct forms are grouped with the Archaeognatha, the most basal of insect groups, and date from the Early Devonian Period. These extinct forms were small creatures, and their three-pronged tail filaments made up most of their length. Archaeognathans most likely fed on detritus such as the dead plant material that covered the floor of their ancient swamp habitats. They could jump-start their movement by flexing their abdomen and jumping. Another indication of their basal design is that they underwent minimal metamorphosis: The young were similar in appearance to the adults.

Silverfish are another wingless insect that probably arose during the Devonian, although definitive specimens do not begin to occur in the fossil record until sediments dating from the Cretaceous Period. Silverfish are classified as zygentomans. They were more flattened than bristletails and were unable to jump.

Odonata: Giant Fliers

Dragonflies and mayflies are among the most ancient winged insects. Early mayflies are known from the Early Carboniferous; the first dragonflies are known from the Late Carboniferous.

Fossil mayflies had secondary wings that were about the same size as the primary wings. This is unlike modern species, in which the second pair of wings is greatly reduced in size. Also unlike their modern descendants, which do not eat, Paleozoic mayflies had sucking mouthparts for extracting juices from plants.

Dragonflies of the Late Paleozoic are known to have reached enormous sizes compared to extant species. *Meganeuropsis*, from Late Carboniferous deposits in Kansas, is the largest known fossil dragonfly. It had a wingspan of 29 inches (74 cm), about as wide as an average refrigerator. Like modern dragonflies, *Meganeuropsis* had two pairs of fixed wings that were held open when the creature was at rest. In *Protohymen*, the two pairs of wings were nearly equal in size, another feature reminiscent of modern dragonflies. One species, *Asthenohymen*, probably could fold its stiff wings back over its abdomen when at rest. In Permian dragonflies, the anatomical features associated with flight began to approach the levels of maneuverability, speed, and hovering demonstrated by modern dragonflies. This leads to the conclusion that these large insects had developed into predators that hunted for smaller insects while flying in the air or clinging to the limbs of trees.

Hemiptera: Sucking Insects

What are known as the "true bugs" or Hemiptera are part of an enormously diverse order with roots going back to the Permian Period. Basal members of this group were probably predators, with mouthparts originally designed to suck fluids from other animals. These same mouthparts were adapted over time to feed on plants, and most hemipterans were, and continue to be, plant eaters. The rise and diversity of the hemipterans coincides with the spread of gymnosperm plants. Extinct members of this group, such as *Archysctina* and *Permopsylla* from the Permian of Kansas, have a moveable beak for piercing and sucking fluids from plants. Two main groups make up the hemipterans: the Sternorrhyncha (aphids, whiteflies, plant lice, and scale insects) and the Auchenorrhyncha (leafhoppers, planthoppers, and cicadas).

The sternorrhynchans lead an immobile life, barely moving from the same spot for their entire lives. They attach themselves to a leaf or stem and remain in place, sometimes in great numbers, creating a harvest of sedentary prey for carnivorous beetles and others insects. Excellent specimens of extinct sternorrhynchans have been found in amber dating from the Jurassic and Cretaceous Periods. Fossil aphids are particularly well known. The earliest specimens of sternorrhynchans appear as wingless nymphs from the Permian and Triassic Periods.

The auchenorrhynchans feed on plant fluids just as do the sternorrhynchans, but the auchenorrhynchans are winged and more mobile. Leafhoppers are known for their extraordinary camouflage, which mimics the stems and leaves on which they feed. Cicadas grow large and have the longest maturation period of any insect. They can fly but live largely static lives, clinging to trees and blending in visually with the bark as they suck plant juices. The earliest fossil auchenorrhynchans are found in sediments dating from the Permian Period.

Orthoptera: Crickets, Katydids, Grasshoppers, and Their Kin

Fossil ancestors of crickets and grasshoppers extend back to the Permian Period and are commonly found in fossil deposits of the Mesozoic Era. This diverse group currently has more than 22,500 species and is divided into two subgroups, the Ensifera (crickets and katydids) and the Caelifera (grasshoppers).

The earliest known ensiferans date from the Late Permian Period; some of the best specimens are found in Mesozoic deposits, particularly from the Early Cretaceous of Brazil. These creatures often are preserved in exquisite detail that includes fully articulated limbs and antennae. Most are not very long, measuring about one inch (25 mm) long or less.

Caeliferans date from the Early Triassic Epoch and are widely known in the Mesozoic and Cenozoic fossil records. Specimens of caeliferans are generally tiny, measuring less than one-half inch (9 mm) long. Extinct insects, including grasshoppers, are sometimes found encased in amber—fossilized tree sap in which the insects were buried alive. Examples from the Dominican Republic

Fossil ancestors of crickets and grasshoppers extend back to the Permian Period and are commonly found in fossil deposits of the Mesozoic Era.

represent several clearly visible specimens with their body parts intact down to the tiny hairs on their legs.

Blattaria: Roaches

Cockroaches were a widely distributed order of insects in the Late Paleozoic. They lived in the damp, dark debris of the forest floor. Early species had the wide, flattened bodies of their extant descendants but were outfitted with much larger wings and a long, external ovipositor, which extended from the posterior. The ovipositor was probably used to insert the insect's eggs into a protective crevice in the ground. The external ovipositor appears in the fossil record of roaches until the Late Jurassic Epoch.

The first roaches lived in the moist swamplands of the Middle Carboniferous. They probably reached their most diverse state during the Carboniferous Period, when the mulch-blanketed floors of tropical forests literally were crawling with them. Considering the supersized state of some other arthropods of the time, it may be surprising to know that early roaches were not all that huge. A typical roach from the Carboniferous, such as *Manoblatta* (from France), was about 1.7 inches (4.3 cm) long. Some exceptions have been found; the largest fossil roach on record is a well-preserved specimen, discovered in 2001, from the Late Carboniferous of Ohio that measures 3.5 inches (9 cm) long.

Coleoptera: Beetles

Living beetles and their grubs are the largest **taxon** of organisms; they make up 40 percent of all insects. Adult beetles are characterized by having two sets of wings; the forewings are armored to cover and protect the rear pair. Beetles generally are flat insects with a hard exoskeleton and jaws designed for biting and chewing.

Most winged insects can be diagnosed by examining the telltale vein pattern of their forewings. This presents a problem with beetles because these insects replaced their forewings with an armored shell. As a result, the fossil record of beetles, although extensive, is sometimes difficult for paleontologists to interpret. Fortunately, the exoskeleton and armor plating of a beetle often is decorated with pits or sculpted surfaces; this gives researchers visible patterns that can be used to compare and associate extinct forms of these creatures.

Ancestors of the beetles appeared in the Early Permian fossil record of Chekarda, in the Ural Mountains of Russia, and in the Czech Republic. The veined forewings of those protobeetles had not yet been completely transformed into an armor shield; instead, the forewing consisted of a long, narrow, leathery shield that was longer than the abdomen. The veins of the forewings made up a distinct pattern of tiny square cells arranged in parallel rows along the insect's length. More fossils of early beetles are found in Late Permian deposits across the supercontinent Pangaea: Specimens have been found in present-day Africa, Australia, Europe, and

Asia. These specimens show some reduction in the leathery, pitted forewings seen in Early Permian examples. The first true beetles, whose veined forewings had been replaced by hardened, veinless forms, lived in the Late Triassic. It is likely that the true beetles first appeared earlier in the Triassic Period, but the fossil record of insects from the Early Triassic has not yet provided evidence of any such **transitional** forms.

Adaptations of Insects

The lifestyle of early insects was immutably linked to the rise and diversification of vascular plants in the Late Paleozoic. Although many groups of living insects feed on plants, there is little evidence that their Paleozoic ancestors did the same. One group, the palaeodictyopteroids, had mouthparts designed for tearing apart loosely packed spore pods or cones or piercing such spore-bearing packets and sucking out the contents. Evidence for this is found in fossils that show the gut of these insects jammed with spores. Some insects also had piercing mouthparts that conceivably could have punctured the skin of a plant to consume its cell juices. Reinforcing the idea that some insect groups had grown dependent on plants for nutrition is the fact that some taxa, including the palaeodictyopteroids, were becoming extinct by the end of the Carboniferous Period, when the once-dominant flora of seed ferns, lycopods, and cordaites diminished substantially in favor of gymnosperms. Those insects became extinct because of their inability to adapt biologically to eating the new kinds of plants.

The world of Paleozoic insects, therefore, was not yet a world of widespread **herbivory**. Plants, however, played an important role in the food chain. Most insects either fed on dead organic matter—such as dead plants, fallen spores, and shed plant parts—or were predatory, feeding on smaller varieties of insects. The ecosystem of the Late Paleozoic created zones of opportunity for plants and animals alike. Crawling insects worked the floor of the tropical forest or climbed the limbs of plants in search of detritus, spores, and sometimes other insects on which to feed. Flying insects sailed among the tallest trees to pick one another off out of the air or to pluck crawling insects from the branches and leaves to which they clung. The largest insects, such as dragonflies with wings measuring up to 29 inches (74 cm) wide, were the largest flying predators of their time and not likely to get eaten by the slow-moving vertebrates that crept along the swamp base. Dragonflies kept their distance from the ground so as not to get tangled in low-growing vegetation.

Insects were the first flying creatures—a most remarkable adaptation that eventually was repeated through the independent evolution of flight in three kinds of vertebrates: pterosaurs, birds, and bats. Just how flight evolved in insects remains a great debate, and two hypotheses have emerged. The first idea, proposed in 1935, suggested that wings **derived** from an advantageous outgrowth of the body wall and did so independently of any preexisting limbs. A more recent hypothesis, first proposed in 1973, is that insect wings were an adaptation of an existing, ancestral appendage, such as gills. Recent work by Michalis Averof and Stephen Cohen of the European Molecular Biology Laboratory in Heidelberg, Germany, makes a compelling case for the gill-origin theory. Averof and Cohen's research identified two genes related to wing-specific functions in insects that are also found in crustaceans. Their theory is that wings evolved from gill-like appendages of a common ancestor of both crustaceans and insects. The evolution of insect flight also benefited from the higher levels of atmospheric oxygen during the Carboniferous Period. Higher atmospheric oxygen levels created denser air, which provided more lift for flying insects.

The subject of the marine origins of insect ancestors and the mention of gills are reminders of yet another anatomical innovation of insects. Insects do not have lungs like fish and other vertebrates. Nor do they have external gills like their marine arthropod ancestors. Insects breathe by a process of gas exchange with the atmosphere. The outside surface of an insect contains several tiny openings that are part of a remarkable **tracheal system** for consuming oxygen. There are two pairs of openings on the insect's thorax and additional openings on each of its other body segments. Each opening or trachea branches into smaller tubes that then branch again to connect directly with an insect's tissues. In this way, energy-providing oxygen is fed directly into the tissues rather than being transported to the tissues by blood as it is in vertebrates. Furthermore, these openings to the outside air can be closed to prevent water loss through evaporation and can be contracted and expanded by the insect to increase or slow down the rate of respiration.

ARACHNIDA: SPIDERS AND SCORPIONS

The arthropod group Arachnida includes the spiders, scorpions, ticks, and their kin. Their heads and thorax are fused and protected by a carapace, or hard outer covering. Arachnids have from zero to four pairs of eyes, eight legs, and a complex set of **anterior** appendages associated with grabbing food, tearing it apart, and preparing it for ingestion.

The appendages used by arachnids for securing food are notoriously effective and deadly. A pair of smaller appendages, called chelicerae, is closest to the mouth. The chelicerae are used to tear food apart. A set of longer appendages, called the pedipalps, is also fixed to the front of the arachnid; these appendages are used to grab and hold food so that it can be torn apart. At the base of these appendages are mandibles, which the animal uses to reduce food to smaller pieces before it is ingested. In scorpions, these appendages generally are covered with a hard protective cover; the pedipalps, which are oversized, terminate with a grasping claw. In spiders, the pedipalps are generally small so as not to interfere with the legs. The pedipalps of spiders sometimes include grappling hooks for securing prey, and the chelicerae of spiders are fangs.

Arachnids have an intriguing evolutionary history. They undoubtedly began as marine creatures that adapted to land. Most living arachnids are terrestrial species. Those living arachnids that live in the water are derived from terrestrial ancestors, so it is clear that some branches of the arachnid family tree returned to the water after having already adapted to life on land.

Eurypterids and Scorpions

Arachnids have roots in the Silurian Period, in the form of aquatic, scorpionlike creatures called eurypterids, or "sea scorpions." The eurypterids are an extinct group of arthropods that lived primarily in brackish freshwater environments and lagoons. Most species were small, but some spectacular examples such as *Pterygotus* routinely reached lengths of more than six feet (1.8 m). Larger still was a fossil specimen of the eurypterid *Jaekelopterus* (Early Devonian, Germany) described in 2007. Based on a single claw, this sea scorpion reached an enormous length of 8.3 feet (2.5 m), the largest known arthropod of all.

The five different families of eurypterids have a superficial resemblance to scorpions and spiders but are more closely related to horseshoe crabs. They have a two-part body consisting of the head and a segmented abdomen. Like arachnids, eurypterids had eight legs, not counting the leglike anterior chelicerae appendages. Eurypterids breathed using gills. The body plan and design of the eurypterid appendages varied widely and radically. In most, but not all, members of this group, the fourth pair of legs was much larger and terminated with paddles. Variations were common, however. The first pair of legs of *Megalograptus,* a eurypterid from the Late Ordovician of Ohio, was long and adorned with sizable spikes for snaring prey. This large species was more than three feet (0.9 m) long; this suggests that it could have preyed on larger arthropods or even on fish that came too close to its aquatic lair. *Pterygotus,* from the Early Devonian of Germany, was about six feet (1.8 m) long and had pincers on its chelicerae appendages. The presence of pincers, however, should not suggest that *Pterygotus* was related to scorpions because scorpion pincers are found on a different pair of appendages. The evolution of pincers in both cases took place independently. Most eurypterids had short legs that would have made terrestrial locomotion implausible, but a few had long, robust legs

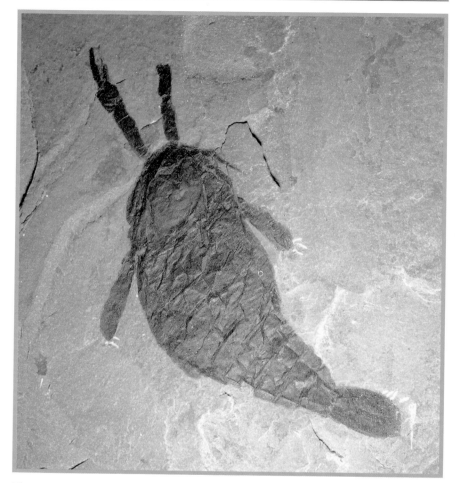

The scorpionlike eurypterid *Pterygotus* from the Early Devonian of Germany reached lengths of six feet (1.8 m) and was a menace to early fish.

that may have allowed them to move about in shallows like modern-day crabs.

Scorpions are members of the arachnid group Scorpiones. The relationship between the first terrestrial arachnids and the eurypterids is not entirely clear. The first true scorpions, such as *Paleophonus* from the Silurian of Sweden, retained gills like those in the eurypterids but had other features that appear to have developed separately from the sea scorpions. In the Middle Paleozoic, gigantic species of eurypterids and aquatic scorpions lived side by side. It would seem that both of these lines of arthropods had a common ancestor from which the two lines split sometime during the Early Silurian.

Gigantism in arthropods had its limitations and disadvantages. It made these animals less capable of supporting their huge bodies with their spindly limbs and probably restricted their radiation to watery habitats. By the Carboniferous Period, formidable—but much smaller—land scorpions are found in the fossil record for the first time. Some of these appear virtually identical to extant species. They range in size up to about 4.5 inches (12 cm) long. Sometime during the Devonian Period, these scorpions developed stronger legs for walking, discarded their gills for a gas-exchange respiratory system similar to that seen in insects, and moved to terrestrial habitats as respectable predatory creatures. Fossils of Late Paleozoic land scorpions are best known from deposits in Illinois, New York, England, Scotland, and the Czech Republic.

Spiders

Spiders are members of the arachnid order Araneae. They are characterized by producing silk, having venom glands with fangs, having eight legs, and lacking wings. Like scorpions, spiders breathe using a gas-exchange system similar to that of insects. Inside the abdomen is a set of flat respiratory grids called book lungs. These are connected to the outside through openings called spiracles. In some species, the spiracles are also connected to a system of tiny tubes called trachea. The trachea or book lungs exchange oxygen directly into the arachnid's tissues without the use of a blood-circulatory system.

The anterior pedipalps and chelicera of spiders are much reduced when compared with those of scorpions. One benefit of having smaller anterior feeding appendages is that they do not interfere

(continues on page 80)

THINK ABOUT IT

400 Million Years Ago in Scotland

One of the most plentiful fossil locations for early terrestrial life is the Rhynie Chert in the north of Scotland. Located near the town of Rhynie, in Aberdeenshire, the site contains fossils from a time when that part of Scotland was located south of the equator, about 400 million years ago. Chert is a quartz-related mineral that occurs naturally from the breakdown of minerals in rocks or decayed organic matter. In the case of the Rhynie Chert, silica deposits literally rained down from geysers or were spread by the action of hot springs to cover and preserve many fine examples of terrestrial plants and arthropods. Most of the plants known from this location probably grew close to the water, where early soils were most common, because the surrounding volcanically active geography was not as welcoming to plant life.

Mining the Rhynie Chert for specimens is quite different from scouting sedimentary rocks for visible signs of fossils. Most of the goodies are locked inside the quartz block and are invisible to the naked eye until examined in a laboratory. The first step in the mining procedure is to use a rock saw to cut a chunk of chert into smaller slices. These slices are then cleaned and polished; this reveals more details within the rock as well as possible signs of organic remains. Because most of the specimens, especially of arthropods, are tiny, a microscope is needed to study them closely. Portions of the larger chert slices that contain specimens are further cut into microscopically thin slices of rock that can be viewed under a microscope. These thin, polished slices of rock are translucent. This allows light to seep through the slices to reveal further detail of the specimens found inside.

Among the many fossils found in the Rhynie Chert are the oldest known insect species, *Rhyniella* and *Rhyniognatha*. As many as 15 species of early terrestrial and near-shore arthropods have been identified in the chert as well as seven species of early land plants.

Fossilization by means of a hot-spring bath preserved dead organisms before they had a chance to decay. This resulted in some remarkable specimens, with exquisite detail down to their very cells. In addition to

Rhynie Scotland, 400 million years ago. Fossils from this location today reveal the nature of the earliest land plants and insects. The area was once subject to frequent volcanic activity.

early insects, the Rhynie Chert also preserved spectacular arthropods called trigonotarbids—ancestors of modern spiders. Most chert insect specimens are quite small in size, with body lengths in the range of one-quarter inch (5 mm). Despite their small size, the chert specimens reveal minute details such as mouthparts, muscle tendons, and respiratory elements of early insects.

Plants of the chert were mostly low-growing sprigs that rarely grew more than eight to 16 inches (20 to 40 cm) tall. *Horneophyton* had upright, leafless, water-conducting branches that bore spores in small, protective,

(continues)

(continued)

cuplike chambers on the branch tips. *Lycopodium* was a short plant with a central trunk covered with scalelike overlapping leaves. One of the first successful upright vascular plants was *Rhynia*, which had a porous covering on its outer stem that moderated water loss while its inner structure of vascularized tissue gave it strength to hold itself up.

British paleontologist Richard Fortey, who specializes in Paleozoic life, remarks that the community of organisms found in the Rhynie Chert is extraordinary not because of "how different they are from their equivalents in the living world," but because of "how remarkably similar" they are. What can be seen in the chert is evidence that plants and animals were living in symbiosis—close, mutually dependent association—nearly as soon as they both ventured out of the water. This mutual dependency is seen today in natural habitats all over the world.

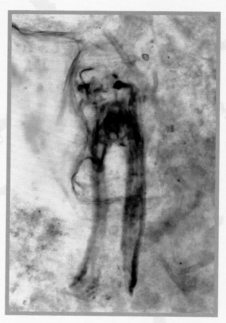

Fragment of the early insect Rhyniognatha shows the large mandibles of the mouth and other parts

(continued from page 77)

with the operation of the spider's frontmost legs. As a result, spiders possess excellent mobility. The pedipalps of spiders often are tipped with a hook for holding prey. The chelicerae are the fangs of the spider; they deliver debilitating venom and help to tear apart the prey. Spiders do not have teeth. After the spider's venom has immobilized its prey, the spider liquefies the prey's insides by injecting enzymes from its own digestive track into the prey. The spider then sucks the soupy meal into itself using the pumping action of its stomach.

Terrestrial spiders clearly evolved from a line of marine arthropod species sometime during the Silurian Period, but their ancestors are a matter of speculation. One extinct, ancestral group of arachnids dating from the Late Silurian and terminating in the Early Permian is the Trigonotarbida. These were not true spiders, as they lacked silk glands and chelicerae equipped with venom glands, but they could have been related to true spiders through a common ancestor. The earliest trigonotarbids date from the Early Devonian deposits of Scotland, Wales, Germany, New York, and Canada.

The true spiders are part of the arachnid group Araneae, which includes more than 40,000 extant species. Within the Araneae are the Mygalomorphae, a group that consists of tarantulas and their closest kin, and the Opisthothelae, a group that includes most common spiders.

Along with the scorpions, spiders and the now-extinct trigonotarbids were among the first land animals. The earliest true spider—with silk glands—is *Attercopus*, found in rocks of Middle Devonian age in Gilboa, New York. This taxon and other early spiders had the silk-spinning spinneret in the middle of the abdomen; this probably limited the use of the silk to such chores as covering a nest or providing a crude, ground-based trap for passing insects. Spiders with a spinneret positioned on the lower abdomen are placed in a special group called the Mesothelae. The Mesothelae were the most common type of spider during the Paleozoic, but only a few species of mesothelids are still living.

The Opisthothelae include the most common types of spiders, with the spinneret placed at the posterior tip of the abdomen. This type of spider first appears in the fossil record about 250 million years ago, at the end of the Permian Period. Having the silk gland positioned at the spider's rear end made it possible for the creature

MAJOR ORDERS OF LAND ARTHROPODS AND THEIR ORIGINS

Arthropod Group	Characteristics	Members	Early Fossil Evidence for Terrestrial Arthropods
Crustaceans	Biting jaws; two-branched appendages; two pairs of antennae	Lobsters, crabs, shrimp, isopods (pill bugs), barnacles	Marine species (Early Cambrian); there were no terrestrial forms during the Paleozoic; pill bugs evolved later, during the Mesozoic Era.
Centipedes and Millipedes	Biting jaws; body consisting of head and numerous body segments; 30-plus single-branched legs	Centipedes, millipedes	Trace fossils of millipede burrows (Late Ordovician) Specimens such as *Casiogrammus* (Middle Silurian, Scotland)
Arachnids	Pincers or fangs for mouthparts; eight legs	Spiders, mites, ticks, scorpions, daddy longlegs	**Scorpions** *Branchioscorpio*, an Early Devonian transitional form with legs for walking on land but aquatic lungs *Archaeophonus* and *Proscorpius* (Late Silurian, New York) **Spiders** Evidence of Middle Devonian spiders exists in the form of a fossil spinneret, the silk-making part of a spider (New York). *Gigantocharinus* (Late Devonian, Pennsylvania) *Eophrynus* (Late Carboniferous, England) (*Anthracomartus* (Late Carboniferous, Poland)
Insects	Biting jaws; six single-branched legs; three body parts; one pair of antennae	Beetles, flies, bees, fleas, true bugs, grasshoppers, butterflies, termites	Proto-insects (Early Devonian) First true insect: *Rhyniella* (Early Devonian, Scotland)

to weave fancy webs and elevate its habitat to the upper branches of ferns and trees, where there were many flying insects to be captured. The posterior spinneret also provided the safety line that a spider uses when it hangs or falls from a high spot.

The tarantulas, or mygalomorphids, also trace their origins to the Late Paleozoic. These are not web-spinning members of the

Araneae. In contrast to the Opisthothelae, mygalomorphids stalk and attack their prey on the ground, sometimes ambushing them. Fossil specimens include probable mygalomorphid trackways from Early Permian sandstone deposits in Arizona.

In the annals of fossil spiders, one might expect there to be a giant or two. In 1980, a fossil arachnid from Late Carboniferous deposits in Argentina temporarily held the world record for the largest spider. The fossil revealed a large, 16-inch (40 cm) body and a leg span of 20 inches (50 cm). This all seemed clear enough to the team of scientists that first examined the specimen, and the creature, dubbed *Megarachne*, or mega-spider, was even given a dubious place of honor in the Guinness Book of World Records. Twenty-five years after its discovery, however, arachnid expert Paul Selden of Manchester University in England had an opportunity to look over the spectacular fossil. To his surprise, he found that it was not a spider at all, but an aquatic animal, probably a euryptid. Selden's certainty was assured. "It has large claws and two big compound eyes," he explained, "whereas spiders normally have eight small eyes. It also appears to have a very robust body or shell with ridges across its back which is not found in any spider known to man." What was once thought to be the largest spider ever known turned out to be a crusty sea scorpion, but an odd one. For the record—that is, the Guinness Book of World Records—the honor of being the world's largest spider fell back to the previous titleholder, a specimen of male goliath bird-eating spider (*Theraphosa*) found in Venezuela in 1965. That specimen had a leg span of 11 inches (28 cm).

SUMMARY

This chapter described the first land animals and the adaptations that made is possible for them to live in a transitional habitat.

1. The first animals to exploit the new terrestrial habitat created by land plants were descendants of marine-based arthropods. Representatives of the different groups of arthropods made

their transitions to land independently, each working out their own unique solutions to living in a dry habitat.

2. Arthropods were particularly adaptable to land because of their tough outer skin covering and thin, jointed appendages that left few soft parts exposed to the evaporative effects of dry air.

3. The first evidence for land animals is found in the form of preserved burrows from the Late Ordovician; these burrows probably were made by ancestral millipedes, the first arthropods to move to land.

4. The earliest fossil evidence of insects comes from the Rhynie Chert deposits of Scotland that date from the Early Devonian. Species included wingless, insectlike springtails and possibly the first winged, true insect.

5. The largest known fossil insect is *Meganeuropsis*, a dragonfly from the Late Carboniferous that had a wingspan of 29 inches (74 cm).

6. Most Paleozoic insects were probably predators and not plant eaters.

7. Insects were the first winged, flying organisms. Insect wings evolved from the gill-like appendages of a common ancestor of both crustaceans and insects.

8. The evolution of gigantism in insects was brought about largely because of richer amounts of oxygen in the Carboniferous atmosphere.

SECTION TWO:
VERTEBRATES ON LAND

4

GOING ASHORE: BECOMING A LAND ANIMAL

About 370 million years ago, a new variety of vertebrates, descended from the lobe-finned fishes, began a cautious migration from the life-sustaining waters of their ancestors, out of the ooze, and onto the rocks and swampy stretches of shoreline that made up the first habitable land. Thus was marked a monumental event in the history of life—a transition that led to the first **amphibians** and to all vertebrate lineages to follow: reptiles, birds, and mammals, including humans.

If the sea was so inviting, and the land was so bare of the necessities of life, one may question why vertebrates ventured onto the land in the first place. The reasons why animals made this monumental move to dry land have been a matter of much scientific speculation. Recently discovered fossil clues to some of the rarest of all fossils—the remains of the earliest land vertebrates—have begun to lead to some consensus among paleontologists who study the evolution of the earliest land creatures. One startling realization made by scientists is that the development of legs and lungs did not occur to enable them to walk out of the water. The development of legs and lungs allowed these creatures to better adapt to their shallow water habitats. This chapter traces the evolutionary adaptations that allowed vertebrates to migrate to a terrestrial habitat and introduces the first vertebrate representatives to make the transition.

ADAPTING TO LIFE ON LAND

The first limbed vertebrates and all of their descendents are members of the vertebrate group **Tetrapoda**. Tetrapods are vertebrate

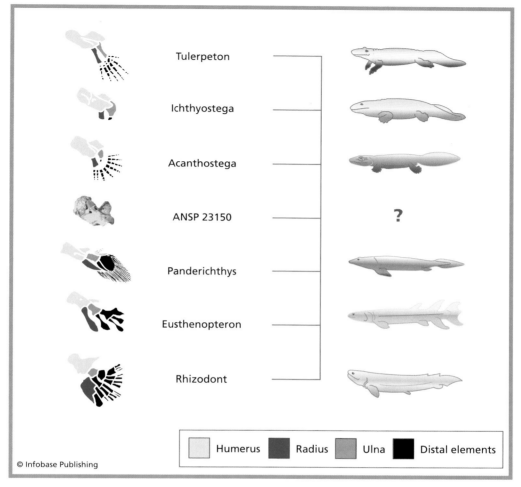

The fossil record provides clues to stages of transformation of the fish fin to the tetrapod limb during the Devonian Period.

animals with four toe-bearing legs. The group also includes two-legged and legless members that are descended from tetrapods.

The first tetrapods descended from fish. The move onto land was not as simple as evolving legs and just leaving the water. Terrestrial habitats were fraught with unique challenges for vertebrates. These pioneers faced many of the same challenges to living on land that plants and arthropods had overcome earlier. These challenges included the adequacy of the creatures' weight-bearing anatomy, the loss of body moisture to the air, the problem of breathing out of the water, sensory adaptation, and reproduction. This section describes the multitude of adaptations that led from fins to feet and to the ability of vertebrates to conquer the land.

Weight-Bearing Anatomy

Without water to support its body weight, a vertebrate out of water had to cope with the stronger pull of gravity while remaining mobile. This adaptation was accomplished through a gradual but complete overhaul of the vertebrate skeleton to maximize its weight-bearing components and limbs.

The transition from fish to four-legged animal did not occur suddenly, but over the course of thousands of generations of many species of creatures. Before the fossil record begins to show unequivocal evidence of animals that could be called tetrapods, there are many examples of evolutionary stages bridging the transformation from fish to limbed animals. Collectively, this evidence shows a progression in skeletal features that led to improved weight-bearing design and other improvements that improved tetrapod adaptation for shallow water and eventually terrestrial life.

Skulls of early tetrapods offer clues to a variety of physiological changes that took place as these creatures adapted to life on land. Compared with the skulls of lobe-finned fishes, the head of the tetrapod gradually became flatter and wider. Changes in the location and size of skull openings point to adaptations for breathing as well as improved eyesight. Nasal passageways developed inside the skull to connect the nostrils to the mouth.

Tetrapod jaws became heftier than those of fish, and the skull grew stronger through a fusing of many of the bones that made up the lighter, more fragile skulls of the tetrapods' fish ancestors. Early tetrapods had two rows of teeth in their lower jaws, as did their fish ancestors. In later tetrapods, however, the teeth of the inner row became smaller, and the teeth of the outer row became larger and fewer than in fish, perhaps marking a transition to feeding on land.

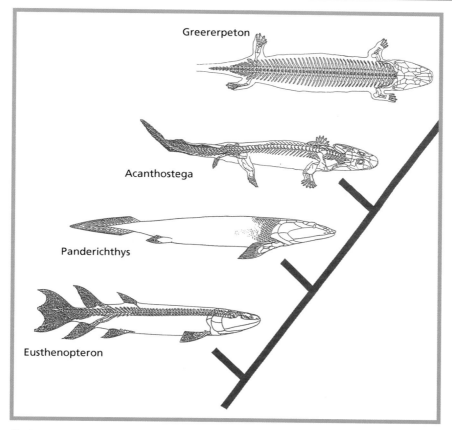

Skeletal modifications that led to land-dwelling tetrapods included the strengthening and repositioning of limbs to be weight-bearing, the addition of limb joints to make terrestrial locomotion possible, and the development of longer trunk ribs to shape and support the body out of the water.

Whereas fish mostly gulp in their food and snag it on their many smaller teeth, tetrapods used their larger outside row of teeth to snag fish and other small prey such as insects. Tetrapods primarily ate fish until well into the Early Carboniferous Period.

The bones at the back of the tetrapod skull became particularly robust, developed a prominent notch, and served as a point of attachment for muscles that allowed the tetrapod to raise its head without moving the rest of the body. This flexible joint between the head and the spine was an innovation of the tetrapods. It allowed

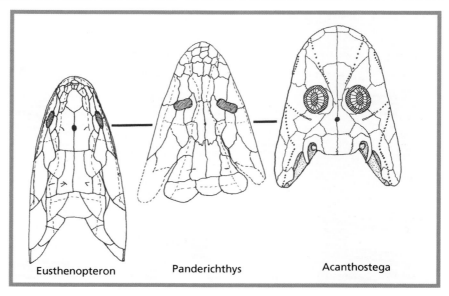

Eusthenopteron   Panderichthys   Acanthostega

The transition from the skull of a fish, such as Eusthenopteron, to that of
a tetrapod, such as Acanthostega, shows that the eyes of early tetrapods
not only became larger than their fish ancestors but began to migrate to
the dorsal surface of the head.

dwellers in shallow waters to raise up their heads to breathe air. It
also led to the development of a flexible neck in many kinds of later
land vertebrates.

The spine, or vertebral column, of the first tetrapods was markedly different from that of lobe-finned fishes. The fish backbone
was not connected to the pelvic girdle, and the individual vertebrae
that made up the spine were simple, lightweight discs that were
fairly uniform in size and contained short, spindly, riblike structures. The tetrapod spine developed stouter, interlocking vertebrae
with sturdy ribs that extended down along the sides of the animal.
The presence of longer ribs in tetrapods is one of the clues that
paleontologists look for when faced with a partial skeleton from the
Devonian that could be from either a fish or a land animal. The vertebral column of the tetrapod was joined to the animal's two pairs
of limbs by pectoral and pelvic girdles; this arrangement provided
strength and flexibility to the body. The tetrapod vertebral column

was strong and capable of supporting the weight of the animal as it walked.

The limbs of the tetrapod were attached to the pelvic and pectoral girdles. The transformation of fins to limbs was of prime importance; it enabled the tetrapod to move around. The limbs and feet had to support the weight of the body while also providing stability for locomotion. The limbs were equipped with another innovation: flexible joints (wrists and ankles) that allowed the animals to maintain balance and traction on uneven terrain. Whereas fish move primarily by undulating the body and tail, tetrapods had to work out a new plan for walking and running on land. One requirement for tetrapod walking is that at least three feet have to be on the ground at the same time. This prevents the animal from losing its balance. Tetrapod locomotion is typified by what is called lateral undulation of the trunk. This is a kind of waddling in which one leg is lifted and moved forward while the other three legs remain in contact with the ground. If one were to look down on a tetrapod and watch it move in slow motion, one would see it lift its left forelimb first, followed by the right hind limb and then followed in turn by the right forelimb and the left hind limb.

The transition from underwater locomotion to walking on land took many interim stages to perfect. In fish, the limbs were shorter and pointed backward from the anterior of the animal. Paleontologist Jennifer Clack of Cambridge University suggests that the earliest tetrapods most likely crawled along on their bellies and used their legs only to pull themselves along or change direction. It was only later that stronger, longer, supporting limbs sprawled out from the sides of the animals and enabled them to walk as amphibians and reptiles walk today.

The limbs of tetrapods owe their evolutionary origins to the lobe-finned fishes, whose bony appendages bore many of the bones that later were maximized for strength and mobility on land. The number of digits (fingers and toes) of the early tetrapods also reveals a period of experimentation in the evolution of these animals. Although five fingers is the rule of thumb for modern tetrapods, even humans, this was not always the formula for success. Clack and her associates have examined a wide range of specimens to show that in the early tetrapods, the number of digits ranged from five to six, seven, and even eight. It is not yet known whether the five-fingered tetrapod evolved from an earlier eight-fingered version, such as *Acanthostega*. What is known is that at some point in the evolution of these animals, those with five fingers managed to survive more often and so outlasted the other varieties. Clack surmises that five fingers turned out to be the optimum number for bearing weight and providing adequate flexibility for walking.

Combating Water Loss

Another key to the survival and continuance of early tetrapods was the adaptation of ways to avoid water loss and the effects of dry air. If there were no fossil evidence available for the earliest land animals, paleontologists might imagine that a successful biological scheme would have been to retain the tough outer covering of **dermal** scales found in these animals' fish ancestors. Curiously, the fossil record disputes this imagined scheme. Remains of the earliest tetrapods show that they were only partially covered with scales, usually on their bellies and probably as a way to protect themselves from scrapes and abrasions while crawling on the ground. The dorsal, or top, side of these earliest tetrapods was not protected by a hard outer covering and probably was more like the soft, moist skin of modern amphibians. While later tetrapods did indeed develop semipermeable skin and even scales to protect against water loss, the earliest tetrapods probably lived their lives in and out of shallow waters and also benefited from a highly humid, moist atmosphere that slowed the effects of desiccation.

Breathing Out of the Water

One major biological challenge for tetrapods was breathing out of the water. The fish ancestors of tetrapods extracted oxygen from the water using gills. Developing a way to extract oxygen from the air required some key anatomical transformations, such as the development of lungs and a way to pump air in and out of them.

The Dipnoi, or lungfishes, were lobe-finned fishes that appeared in the Early Devonian. Although lungfish were more primitive than the Osteolepiformes, the group of lobe-finned fishes from which tetrapods evolved, it is surmised that lobe-finned fishes had developed respiratory innovations to allow them to breathe air in shallow water habitats. Most fishes have a swim bladder to keep them buoyant in the water. Lungfishes—and probably the osteolepiforms, too—had a primitive lung from which the swim bladder was derived.

Modern tetrapods use two forms of breathing. **Costal ventilation** is most common; it uses abdominal muscles and the rib cage to expand and contract the lungs, forcing air in and out. This form of respiration is found in all amniotes. Another form of respiration is that of **buccal pumping,** seen in lungfishes and amphibians such as frogs and salamanders. During buccal pumping, air is sucked into the throat and then squeezed down the throat into the lungs by raising the floor of the mouth.

Fossil evidence suggests that the earliest tetrapods were probably buccal pumpers. Their wide mouths and broad heads would have provided increased volume for moving air in and out of their lungs. They evidently did this without the aid of abdominal muscles and ribs because these features were much reduced in early tetrapods. The high concentration of oxygen in the Devonian and Carboniferous atmosphere would certainly have aided their adaptation to land by fueling their bodies more fully with every breath than is the case with today's land animals.

In time, most land animals drifted to a system of costal ventilation. Clack suggests that this transition, except in the true amphibians and extant lungfishes, probably occurred in three stages as land animals diversified. The first stage would have been buccal pumping only. The second stage would have engaged abdominal muscles only for exhalation. The third stage, achieved by the amniotes, used muscles for breathing in and breathing out.

Sensory Capacity

Seeing and hearing underwater is markedly different from seeing and hearing on land. Anybody who has swum underwater knows this. Humans' eyes and ears are not optimized for seeing or hearing underwater. The early tetrapods faced the opposite challenge. To survive effectively on land, tetrapods had to develop changes to the way they saw and heard the world outside of the aquatic domain of their fish ancestors.

In reptiles and amphibians, hearing is reliant on a middle-ear bone called the **stapes**. This tiny bone amplifies vibrations from the eardrum, or tympanic membrane, and transmits them to the inner ear, where the brain can detect them. Fossils of the earliest tetrapods and of closely related lobe-finned fishes such as *Eusthenopteron* and *Panderichthys* provide evidence of the transformation of this bone from fish ancestors. The most likely scenario for the change is that the stapes evolved as a bony modification of a jaw-hinging structure around the same time that fins were beginning to transform into limbs with digits. By the time of the eight-fingered *Acanthostega*, about 20 million years later, this tiny skull bone had acquired the functionality of a primitive terrestrial ear. It probably was sensitive only to lower-frequency sounds, however, because of its bulky design and lack of a tympanic membrane of appreciable size. The early mammals were the first to evolve a larger eardrum that was good for hearing high-frequency sounds carried by the air.

The evolution of terrestrial vision most likely occurred in the Late Devonian, at about the same time that hearing began to adjust to air and tetrapods improved their ability to walk on land. The earliest tetrapods most likely spent much of their time in shallow streams and ponds, resting partially underwater much of the time. Changes took place over many generations of these animals to improve their ability to see, hear, breathe, and protect themselves from desiccation. It can be seen in the fossil record that the eyes of early tetrapods not only became larger than the eyes of their fish ancestors, but also began to migrate to the dorsal surface of the head. This gave the tetrapod the ability to lie on the bottom in shallow water while surveying for prey, and to look up out of the water while only partially exposing itself. Over millions of years, the lenses of the eyes modified ever so gradually to become optimized for seeing in the air. This probably occurred by the Late Devonian and coincided with a suite of biological improvements to locomotion, the senses, respiration, and water retainment that made tetrapods better equipped to remain outside of the water for longer periods of time.

There is little fossil evidence related to the sense of smell of the early tetrapods. One difference between fish and tetrapods is that a fish uses the nose only to detect smells, while a tetrapod uses the nose for breathing as well as for smelling. Available fossils show no significant difference between the nostrils of lobe-finned fishes and the nostrils of the earliest tetrapods. This leads to an assumption that the nose was used only for smelling. As Jennifer Clack points out, however, sampling the air for smells was probably a first step toward inhaling air for breathing.

Reproduction

Success on land also required tetrapods to find a way to reproduce. With virtually no fossil evidence of reproductive strategies, it is assumed by most paleontologists that the first tetrapods were most similar in this regard to today's amphibians. Amphibians such as frogs and salamanders must lay their eggs in water, where the young hatch as fully aquatic, gill-breathing tadpoles. Evidence of fossil tadpoles from the Carboniferous confirms that some early tetrapods reproduced in this manner. The young hatched in the water as tadpoles and breathed through gills until they underwent a metamorphosis and took on the four-legged form of adults.

FROM FINS TO LEGS

Until about 20 years ago, a scarcity of tetrapod fossils led paleontologists to make several basic assumptions about the evolution of the first land animals. Central to an interpretation of tetrapod origins was the idea that legs developed as a means for walking on land. This idea made sense based on the timing of known fossil specimens and the best information available about the specimens' ancient habitats. These basic assumptions have changed dramatically in recent years due to a renaissance of tetrapod fossil discoveries. These recent discoveries have broadened the time span of the tetrapods' earliest development and have provided more data about the kinds of environments in which the animals thrived.

To understand the evolution of ideas surrounding the transition of fishes to tetrapods, it is instructional to explore the theories of paleontologist Alfred S. Romer (1894–1973), a pioneering thinker in this field. Romer was an innovative researcher who combined knowledge from vertebrate paleontology, comparative anatomy, and embryology to form a more broadly informed understanding of extinct vertebrates. One of his special areas of interest was the evolution of the first land vertebrates from fishes. In exploring this field, Romer questioned many of the once-accepted reasons for the migration of backboned animals from sea to land.

During the 1960s, Romer was at the center of the debate about the origin of terrestrial animals. At that time, several theories about the development of the first land vertebrates were being debated. One suggestion was that an increasing abundance of atmospheric oxygen lured animals from the sea to the land. Romer objected to this theory because some lungfishes of the Paleozoic had already developed air-breathing lungs and "could obtain all the atmospheric oxygen they wished by merely sticking their heads out of water." Hence, venturing onto land was unnecessary for them.

Another theory about the movement of vertebrates to the land was that some species were escaping the ocean to avoid predators. Romer also discounted this idea; he reminded his colleagues that the closest relatives of the first tetrapods—the lobe-finned fishes—were generally considered to be aggressive predators in their own right and not likely to be forced out of many habitats for this reason.

Other paleontologists of Romer's time believed that the key to the mystery of migration to land was linked to food sources. In the opinion of these scientists, the mere opportunity to acquire new food sources on land was enough to effect the steady but slow adaptation of some fishes to onshore habitats. Once again, this theory did not satisfy Romer. He argued that because the first land vertebrates were predators, they were unlikely to have found suitable prey in large enough numbers during the Late Devonian Period. Romer's objection made perfect sense in the 1960s because it was thought at that time that insects and other small invertebrates were not widely available during the Late Devonian.

Underlying all of Romer's objections to the then-prevalent theories about the migration of vertebrates to land was that such explanations were not based on the anatomical and physiological realities of the animals in question; rather, they were based on "urges or directives" that caused the animals to seek life out of the oceans. In response to the prevailing theories, in 1968, Romer presented a well-conceived theory about taking to land that was based on asking a biological question about these land-seeking creatures: "Can such an explanation be found for the development in fishes of such terrestrially useful structures as lungs and legs?"

Romer answered his own question with an emphatic, "Yes." He found reasons why some fishes could have developed adaptations such as lungs and legs to improve their chances for survival, even if they were purely water dwellers. His explanation? Lungs and legs would have been important to the survival of fishes caught in shallow waters during times of drought. This would have been particularly important to freshwater species that lived in ponds, lakes, and streams that were subject to periodic dry spells. Lungs and primitive limbs in the form of pectoral fins would have enabled fishes to survive temporarily in shallow, stagnant water, or even out of the water, by allowing the fishes to breathe and to move across a muddy, drying streambed or pond to reach the water again. Such fishes certainly were doomed if water did not return in a reasonable time to reinstate their watery habitat, but these adaptations nonetheless made sense even in the absence of a migration to dry land on a full-time basis. This explanation was the key to the way in which Romer believed that amphibians evolved from lobe-finned fishes. Over time, in those cases in which both lobe-finned fishes and the earliest amphibians were victimized by drought, it would be the amphibians' ability to get up and walk away to a nearby stream or pond that would gradually select them as the progenitors of all land creatures that followed. The survival of early tetrapods in those circumstances led to the continuance of their anatomical traits in vertebrates that followed.

Although lungs and legs made life on land possible, Romer concluded that both of those adaptations had not evolved "in some mystic drive or urge toward a career on land" but had arisen "as structures useful in enabling a water dweller to survive as a water dweller." Romer suggested this premise more than 40 years ago; however, as intriguing as the idea was, it was not supported by much fossil evidence. In fact, the fossil record has a significant gap at the very place where Romer's idea might best be proved. The first known tetrapods—*Ichthyostega* and *Acanthostega*—date from about 365 million years ago, in the Late Devonian Period. Following the Late Devonian and extending into the Carboniferous is a gap of about 30 million years in the fossil record between those earliest known tetrapods and the tetrapods that are known from later in the Carboniferous. This span came to be known as "Romer's Gap," in part because of Romer's own tireless efforts to fill the gap with new fossil evidence. This 30 million-year void in the fossil evidence of early land vertebrates was significant because it was during that span that tetrapods fully developed many of the key anatomical traits that made life on land possible: legs, lungs, supporting skel-etal structures, and the eyes and ears necessary for interpreting the world outside of the water.

A spurt of fossil discoveries since about 1990 has begun to fill Romer's Gap, shedding light on the critical transition of fish to tet-rapod. The transition from fish to tetrapod did not proceed along a simple straight-line of adaptation; it now appears that some extinct lobe-finned fishes had limblike fins with skeletal features similar to those seen in tetrapods. One such fish specimen is *Sauripterus*, described by Ted Daeschler of the Academy of Natural Sciences of Philadelphia and Neil Shubin of the University of Chicago and which was found in sedimentary rocks of Late Devonian age in Pennsylvania. The limb elements of this specimen contain many fish and tetrapod features, including paddlelike fin rays and a tetrapodlike internal fin skeleton.

In 1987, Jennifer Clack and her associates discovered the best specimen yet of the early tetrapod *Acanthostega*. Their discovery revealed that this animal, considered to be one of the first tetrapods, was in reality poorly equipped for life on land. Its limbs were punier than originally surmised and lacked the kind of wrist and ankle joints necessary to maneuver effectively on land. *Acanthostega* most certainly had lungs, but its short rib cage suggests that it relied on buccal ventilation rather than on breathing powered by abdominal muscles. *Acanthostega* also had gills; this suggests that it still had not completely made the transition from water to land. Its tail was decidedly long, vertically flattened, and rayed like that of a lobe-finned fish. These features paint a picture of *Acanthostega* different from what had been envisioned originally. Rather than being primarily a land-dwelling creature, *Acanthostega* most likely was a water dweller with paddlelike legs. It spent much of its time lying in shallow waters, where it could view the outside world with its dorsally positioned eyes and occasionally take a breath of air.

An understanding of the kinds of environments that once hosted Devonian tetrapods also has grown with the discovery of more specimens around the world. Key fossil localities are still somewhat scarce, but they are spread across the globe; they include Greenland, Russia, Quebec, Pennsylvania, Estonia, Latvia, New South Wales, and northwestern China. Tetrapods appear to have originated in environments that were not strictly marine but instead featured a combination of freshwater and saltwater. The climates associated with early tetrapods include extreme tropics subject to monsoonal winds and also more temperate subtropics.

Leaving the Water

Now, having seen that fish did not come out of the water before they developed legs and lungs, one can return to the original question about why vertebrates left the water to begin with. A likely explanation is that for animals that could breathe and move outside of the water, the land represented a rich, new, uncharted domain. By the Late Devonian Epoch, both saltwater and freshwater habitats were populated by an abundance of fishes. Competition in the water was predicated by size: No matter how big a fish was, there was probably a bigger fish that could eat it. Early tetrapods were still primarily aquatic, and their main food source was certainly fish. The ability of tetrapods to maneuver effectively in shallow water systems or to cross land to reach other pools was critical to their success because in these habitats they had virtually no competition for fish prey. As tetrapods became increasingly terrestrial, they found themselves to be the largest land predators. They benefited from the greening of the world by living in the safe shadows of plants, breathing the oxygen-rich air enriched by plants, and profiting from the lush, moist habitat the enabled them to lurk effectively for prey.

Arthropods, including insects, may also have been a source of tetrapod food. By the Middle Carboniferous Period, there is fossil evidence that insects had begun to eat plants, a development that not only expanded the diversity of insects, but also expanded the primary food source for tetrapods. By the Late Carboniferous, some vertebrates developed a taste for plants, further extending their domain in the direction of an alternative food source that was available in virtually unlimited quantities. Tetrapods left the water, therefore, to occupy a largely untapped habitat that they could easily dominate.

Chapter 5 continues this discussion by presenting fossil evidence for the successful transition of tetrapods from the water to the land.

SUMMARY

This chapter traced the evolutionary adaptations that allowed vertebrates to migrate to a terrestrial habitat and introduced the first vertebrates to make the transition.

1. The first limbed vertebrates and all of their descendents are members of the vertebrate group Tetrapoda—animals with four toe-bearing legs.

2. Tetrapods overcame several anatomical and physiological challenges to living out of the water by evolving adaptations to improve their weight-bearing anatomy, their water retention, their respiration, their senses, and their reproductive strategies.

3. The limbs of tetrapods were an adaptation of vertebrates that still lived in the water; these limbs presumably provided a means for animals living in shallow water to move through swampy ecosystems and also enable them to lay in wait and ambush prey.

4. Limbs of waterborne animals had the additional advantage of allowing them to lift their heads out of the water to breathe air, a critical step in the move toward living on land.

5. Tetrapods eventually left the water to occupy a largely untapped habitat that they could easily dominate.

▼
5

THE DIVERSITY
OF EARLY TETRAPODS

The first vertebrates to develop limbs began a transformation toward terrestrial life that profoundly changed the course of evolution and ecosystems on land. It was a time of evolutionary opportunity and of experimentation in several directions, as animals adapted to meet the requirements of life in shallow stream systems and eventually on land. This chapter begins with the first limbed animals and then explores the great diversity of early tetrapods that flourished during the latter half of the Paleozoic Era.

BASAL DEVONIAN TETRAPODS

In the history of life, there are few evolutionary transformations to rival the impact of the development of land vertebrates from lobe-finned fishes. The fossil evidence for the evolutionary origins of tetrapods has been greatly enriched in recent years. The most important extinct representatives found during three overlapping stages of tetrapod evolution are as follows:

- Lobe-finned fishes (416 to 375 million years ago). These fully aquatic fishes exhibit some traits associated with early tetrapods. Lobe-finned fishes did not become extinct 375 million years ago, but although they were a diverse group in the Devonian Period, the coelacanth and lungfishes are the only lobe-finned fish still living. The lobe-finned fishes discussed here are those that are closely related to the first tetrapods.

- Near-terrestrial tetrapods (385 to 360 mya). These are specific taxa that exhibit some tetrapod traits but that probably lived mostly in the water. Their limbs were short and paddlelike.
- Early tetrapods (365 to 360 mya). These were increasingly terrestrial vertebrates with limbs and other traits adapted for land that did not exhibit clearly fishlike traits such as fins, gills, or paddlelike limbs. They were still primarily aquatic.

The earliest traces of basal tetrapods come in the form of partial-body fossils and **trackways** that date from the latter part of the Devonian, about 380 million years ago. Most of these partial specimens were so fragmentary that they did not readily reveal their tetrapod origins. Consisting mostly of lower jaw fragments and a few limb elements, fossils that included parts of *Obruchevicthys* (Latvia and Russia) and *Elginerpeton* (Scotland) were originally considered to be sarcopterygians, or lobe-finned fishes. These enigmatic specimens rested for many years in museum drawers in Europe until discoveries of additional remains of Late Devonian tetrapods encouraged scientists to take a closer look at the older specimens. Swedish paleontologist Per Ahlberg was instrumental in reinvestigating *Obruchevicthys* and *Elginerpeton* during the 1990s, establishing them as the two oldest tetrapods known from the fossil record. No feet or fins are known for these animals, but their jaws share many traits of tetrapods. The shape and length of their jaws are distinctive enough to suggest that *Obruchevicthys* and *Elginerpeton* were part of a short-lived branch of the early radiation of tetrapods. Ahlberg estimated that *Elginerpeton* was about five feet (1.5 m) long. Two additional Late Devonian specimens known only from fragments include *Livoniana* (Latvia) and *Elpistostege* (Canada), each of which hints at a transitional stage between the lobe-finned fishes and the tetrapods.

Several trackways from the Late Devonian have been referred to early tetrapods. The most notable come from the Genoa River area in Australia and include two sets of tracks. One set shows an animal that was dragging its tail. The other set includes no evidence of either a tail or belly drag; this suggests that the animal was walking. Unfortunately, it cannot be determined whether these tracks were left underwater or on dry ground, so it cannot be said with certainty that they were made by a walking or floating tetrapod.

Lobe-Finned Fishes

Lobe-finned fishes—the sarcopterygians—rose during the Early Devonian Period and were the first dominant group of bony fishes. Their numbers dwindled by the end of the Paleozoic with the rise of the ray-finned fishes, but not before some members of this group evolved to become the first limbed vertebrates. Four groups of sarcopterygians are recognized.

- *Porolepiformes*: an early group of sarcopterygians, now extinct.
- *Osteolepiformes*: advanced group of sarcopterygians, now extinct, although they are the ancestral roots to land animals.
- *Actinistia*: the coelacanths, the only marine form of lobe-finned fishes that survives to this day.
- *Dipnoi*: the lungfishes, which are still represented by three living freshwater species.

Of these groups, the osteolepiforms appear to be the best link between fishes and terrestrial vertebrates. These fishes had a more efficient arrangement of fins than the porolepiforms, with the osteolepiforms' fins concentrated more toward the midpoint of the animals' long body than the porolepiforms'. An early clue to the evolution of tetrapods is also seen in the consolidation of anterior skull bones in the osteolepiforms. In more basal lobe-finned fishes and lungfishes, the bones of the snout were an unpatterned mosaic of many small bones. With early osteolepiforms such as *Osteolepis* (Middle Devonian, Scotland), these bones had already begun to consolidate into the more fused and robust pattern seen in tetrapods. Following are representative sarcopterygians.

Eusthenopteron (Late Devonian). Fossils of *Eusthenopteron* have been found in Late Devonian rocks in many parts of the world, but

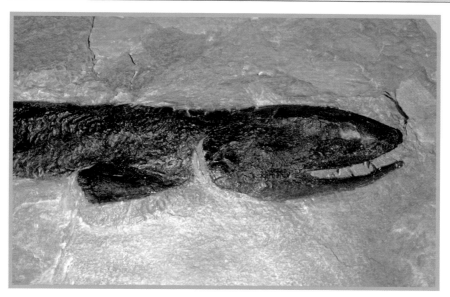

Eusthenopteron was likely an aquatic ancestor of tetrapods.

the animal is best known from Miguasha, Canada. It was a large fish, measuring up to four feet (1.2 m) long. Several intriguing anatomical features make *Eusthenopteron* an excellent candidate for an aquatic relative of tetrapods. Most importantly, the bones of its pectoral and pelvic fins include many of the important features that would be needed by a walking creature, giving it ancestral arms and legs in the form of fins. Other features that unite *Eusthenopteron* with early land animals include the makeup of its teeth, the design of its spine, and the arrangement of bones in the front of the skull.

Tiktaalik (Late Devonian). One of the newest specimens to be added to the list of transitional fish-tetrapods, *Tiktaalik* was described in April 2006 by Ted Daeschler. Working in the Canadian Arctic, Ted Daeschler, Neil Shubin, Farish Jenkins, and their team recovered three partial skeletons and many isolated elements of this startling fish that represents a key stage in the transition of fish to land. A composite of the three specimens provides abundant information about most of the front half of the fish, including remarkably complete skulls, pectoral girdles, and front fins, all preserved in their original articulated position. The suite of skeletal features shows that *Tiktaalik* was clearly a fish with adaptations for life in shallow aquatic ecosystems and perhaps for staying out of the water for short periods of time. Its body and head were flat, with eyes on top, reminiscent of crocodiles. Its nostrils were on the side of its head, closer to the mouth, like other transitional fish-tetrapods. Its ribs were wider than those of a fish, suggesting that *Tiktaalik* was somewhat capable of supporting its weight out of the buoyant medium of water. *Tiktaalik* had a neck, a feature not seen in true fish but one essential for an animal that must lift its head out of the water to breathe air; the neck also is essential to provide an animal with sufficient flex and mobility while walking on land. The skull includes evidence of gills for breathing in water as well as structures that would have aided buccal pumping as in early amphibians. *Tiktaalik* is even more evolutionarily significant because of its front fins, which had bones similar to those in the forelimb and wrist of a tetrapod. The wrist design of *Tiktaalik* has great affinities with elements that still can be seen in land animals today. Neil Shubin explains that *Tiktaalik* "tells us to a great extent how parts of our own skeleton evolved."

The geology of the Arctic site where *Tiktaalik* was recovered shows that the environment was that of a small stream in a tropical or subtropical river delta. *Tiktaalik* was most at home in shallow waters, where it probably rested in wait for passing fish and arthropods that it could snap up with its formidable jaws. Its flexible neck, respiratory options, limblike fins, and enlarged rib cage suggest that *Tiktaalik* could have thrived as a shallow-water predator while also leaving the water on occasion to exploit its opportunities on land.

This remarkable creature, heralded as a missing link of sorts in the world of tetrapod discoveries, demonstrates that shallow-water habitats were the evolutionary proving ground for the first tetrapods. The term *missing link* is misleading, however, because it suggests that *Tiktaalik* is the direct ancestor of tetrapods—something that cannot be known from the fossil record. "*Tiktaalik* is a link," says Daeschler. "It certainly was missing. But there are plenty more links to find in any evolutionary sequence." *Tiktaalik's* combination of fish and tetrapod features makes it somewhat difficult to classify, but it represents precisely the kind of animal that paleontologists would expect to find as a diverse group of many families of fishes gradually evolved an affinity for living on land. "Evolution proceeds slowly," explains Daeschler. "It proceeds in a mosaic pattern with some elements changing while others stay the same."

Panderichthys (Mid to Late Devonian). Two species of *Panderichthys* are known from several excellent specimens found in Latvia and Russia. At three to four feet (1 to 1.5 m) long, the animal was an inhabitant of coastal swamps and lagoons. This taxon also represents a transitional form between waterborne fishes and tetrapods, though it does not show several of the tetrapodlike features seen in *Tiktaalik*. *Panderichthys* is distinguished from its contemporary *Eusthenopteron* by a lack of dorsal fins and a much more tetrapod-like fin structure. Its skull was long and flattened, and the eyes were located toward the top of the head. Both of these traits are seen in later tetrapods.

Near-Terrestrial Tetrapods

This category includes taxa that are not quite fully terrestrial yet probably not exclusively aquatic as are most sarcopterygian fish. The animals mentioned below are grouped with the tetrapods because of the development of their skulls and because they possess a generalized set of limbs with digits. The distinction made here between near-terrestrial tetrapods and tetrapods is one of degree: These animals represent an important transitional stage in the evolution of land vertebrates but also appear better suited for life in shallow waters.

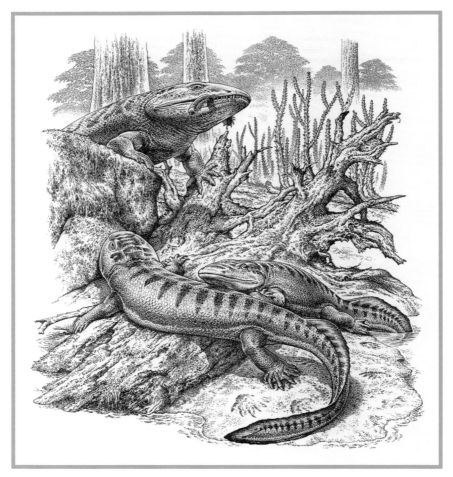

Ichthyostega (top) and Acanthostega (bottom). Ichthyostega was very much at home in the water, even though it did not have gills. Its limbs were more robust than Acanthostega and its abdomen was fortified with long, thick, overlapping ribs.

Acanthostega (Late Devonian). The first fossil evidence of *Acanthostega* included only fragments of the skull roof that were collected in Greenland in 1933. The Greenland specimen was not scientifically described until 1952, when Swedish paleontologist Erik Jarvik assessed it as an early tetrapod. *Acanthostega* comes from the same geological units that also yielded the tetrapod *Ichthyostega*, a taxon with which Jarvik was intimately familiar. Fossil evidence for *Acanthostega* remained scant until 1987, when a joint Swedish-British expedition recovered enough remaining fossil material to reconstruct nearly the entire skeleton.

Although *Acanthostega* originally was thought to be more terrestrial than aquatic, the newer evidence painted a different picture of this basal tetrapod. Paleontologist Jennifer Clack, a participant in the 1987 fossil expedition, has studied the specimen extensively; she characterizes it as an anatomical intermediary between lobe-finned fishes and fully terrestrial tetrapods. *Acanthostega* clearly had legs and feet rather than fins, but the legs were short and paddlelike. Other aquatic features—including gills, a fishlike spine, and short ribs—strongly suggest that *Acanthostega* spent most of its time in the water.

This recent interpretation of *Acanthostega* as a waterbound tetrapod has revolutionized scientific thought about the evolution of limbs. Here was a tetrapod with legs and feet rather than fins that probably lived in the water; this suggests that limbs provided an advantage to these animals prior to learning to walk on land. Clack and her colleague Michael Coates suggest that one stage in the evolution of tetrapods was the animals' use of legs to prop themselves up in the shallow water, possibly while lying in wait for prey or poking their heads out into the air.

Ventastega (Late Devonian). Another fragmentary but key early tetrapod taxon that languished in museum drawers for years is *Ventastega,* from Latvia. The fossil evidence consists of a partial skull with jaws and some postcranial elements, including fragments of collarbone, forearm, shoulder, pelvis, ribs, and tail. The skull and jaws are similar to those of *Acanthostega,* with the addition of paired, fanglike teeth. This is a trait normally associated with fish and suggests that *Ventastega* may be a more primitive tetrapod than *Acanthostega* and probably shared the latter's affinity for the water.

Unnamed specimen ANSP 21350. (Late Devonian). Another specimen that has figured large in the debate over the development of tetrapod limbs consists only of a single humerus (upper front leg bone). It was found in a fossil-rich site in north-central Pennsylvania known as Red Hill, a road cut where research is conducted by the Academy of Natural Sciences of Philadelphia (ANSP). The site represents a floodplain from about 365 million years ago and includes shallow-channel and channel-margin environments rich with fossils of fishes, plants, and occasional fragments of tetrapods. The specimen known simply as "ANSP 21350" was recovered by Daeschler and an ANSP field crew and described in 2004 by Daeschler and Neil Shubin. The three-inch (7.5 cm) arm bone is important because it shows a pattern of ridges to which strong pectoral muscles were once attached, as well as a well-developed elbow joint. These features suggest that this particular early tetrapod could prop its body up in the manner of *Acanthostega*, though probably mostly in an aquatic setting.

Early Tetrapods

The discovery of *Ichthyostega* in 1932 pushed back the known origin of tetrapods to the Late Devonian. Prior to that, the earliest known tetrapods were the much more derived and amphibianlike specimens from the Carboniferous. The discovery of *Ichthyostega* provided some excellent clues to the early adaptation of lobe-finned fishes to life on land, but the discovery presented some puzzles as well.

While some Carboniferous tetrapods were clearly optimized for living on land, those of the Late Devonian appeared to consist of a hodgepodge of fish and tetrapod features. What had previously been viewed as the relatively straight-line evolution of legs so that animals could walk on land has now been clouded by the realization that the first animals with legs probably rarely left the water.

Ichthyostega (Late Devonian). *Ichthyostega* is known from several excellent specimens and was the first taxon to push back the origin of tetrapods to the Late Devonian. As such, *Ichthyostega* is often thought of as the archetype of all early tetrapods, even though other specimens such as the much less complete *Tulerpeton* feature somewhat more derived traits found in later tetrapods. In truth, *Ichthyostega* was very much at home in the water, although it did not have gills. Its limbs were more robust than those of *Acanthostega*, and its abdomen was fortified with long, thick, overlapping ribs. Its spine was fishlike but differed from that of *Acanthostega* by possessing bony projections called zygapophyses; these projections served as points for muscle attachment to strengthen the body. The hefty limbs, robust ribs, and sturdy spine enabled *Ichthyostega* to support its body while on land and to walk stiffly, if not nimbly.

Known specimens of *Ichthyostega* do not yet show the presence of wrists or ankles, but the animal had seven digits on each of its feet. The **hind limbs** were considerably shorter than the front limbs; this suggests that the back legs were probably used for paddling in the water and the front legs for propping the animal up and walking on land using the tetrapod equivalent of front-wheel drive. *Ichthyostega* was moderately large; it measured about four feet (1.2 m) long. Its skull was broad and flattened, with orbits for the eyes positioned on the top of the skull. *Ichthyostega*'s teeth were remarkably different from the short teeth of *Acanthostega*. The upper jaw of *Ichthyostega* had an outer row of long, conical teeth and an inner row of smaller teeth. The bottom jaw had only a row of smaller teeth. These teeth might have given *Ichthyostega* many types of prey to choose from, including fish, aquatic and terrestrial arthropods, and perhaps other tetrapods. Like *Acanthostega*, *Ichthyostega* was probably at home in the water; however, its sturdier, less fishlike skeleton and its lack of gills suggest that it was also at home on land.

Tulerpeton (Late Devonian): Recovered from a fossil site near Tula, Russia, *Tulerpeton* is known from less-complete skeletal elements than either *Acanthostega* or *Ichthyostega* but is nonetheless significant because of what those few elements reveal. The remains include a forelimb, a hind limb, part of the shoulder girdle, a piece of jaw, and bony belly scales, called scutes, that protected *Tulerpeton* from scraping against the ground. As with *Ichthyostega*, this tetrapod had a peculiar number of digits: six. Clearly, by the Late Devonian, tetrapods had not yet settled on five as the optimum number of digits, as seen in the Carboniferous. The shoulder bones and longer forelimbs of *Tulerpeton* are more suited for life on land than those in either *Acanthostega* or *Ichthyostega*, and it is assumed that *Tulerpeton* was capable of terrestrial locomotion. *Tulerpeton*'s hind limbs, however, lacked a true ankle and probably were also good at paddling in the water; this shows once again that tetrapods from the Late Devonian were still undergoing evolutionary changes that would free them from the water.

The above specimens, although fragmentary, represent the most complete fossil material of Devonian tetrapods currently known. The paleontology of Devonian tetrapods is remarkably limited when it comes to the abundance of specimens. For those who study the very earliest forms of tetrapods, a highly valued fossil specimen often amounts to no more than a single jaw or leg bone. A postscript should therefore be made regarding several even less informative partial specimens that have affinities with tetrapods but about which little more can accurately be surmised. If they say nothing else, these partial specimens speak to the worldwide distribution and diversity of early tetrapods and proclaim the hope that more discoveries are imminent—discoveries that will help complete the story of the first Devonian limbed vertebrates. Most of these specimens were described during the past 12 years and include the pectoral girdle and jaw of *Hynerpeton* (Red Hill, Pennsylvania), the first tetrapod found in the United States; the jaw of *Densignathus* (Red Hill, Pennsylvania); *Jakubsonia* (Russia), known from a partial jaw bone and upper shoulder; and *Metaxygnathus* (New South Wales, Australia) and *Sinostega* (northwest China), both known only from lower jaw fragments and the first such early tetrapod specimens from their respective parts of the world.

By the end of the Devonian Period, the first limbed vertebrates had begun to find their niche in the river floodplains of a greening world. Their existence was not entirely divorced from the aquatic habitat of their ancestors, and they certainly spent much of their life in the water, particularly for feeding and reproduction. This was a workable scheme in the humid, rain-drenched world in which these creatures lived, and it gave rise to an increasingly diverse variety

LATE DEVONIAN LOBE-FINNED FISHES, BASAL TETRAPODS AND THEIR LOCATIONS

Locality	Age*	Taxon/Taxa	Classification
Eastern Greenland	Famennian	*Acanthostega* *Ichthyostega*	Early tetrapod
Red Hill, Pennsylvania, United States	Famennian	*Densignathus* *Hynerpeton*	Early tetrapod
Ellesmere Island, Canada	Early to Middle Frasnian	*Tiktaalik*	Lobe-finned fish
Scat Crag, Scotland	Late Frasnian	*Elginerpeton*	Early tetrapod
Escuminac Bay, Quebec, Canada		*Elpistostege*	Lobe-finned fish
Oryl Region of Russia	Lower Famennian	*Jakubsonia*	Early tetrapod
Guaha Formation of Latvia and Estonia border area	Late Givetian, Late-Middle Devonian or Early Frasnian, Early-Late Devonian	*Livoniana* *Panderichthys*	Lobe-finned fishes
New South Wales, Australia	Frasnian-Famennian boundary to the Late Famennian	*Metaxygnathus*	Early tetrapod
Eastern Latvia	Late Frasnian	*Obruchevichthys*	Early tetrapod
Ningxia Hui Autonomous Region, northwest China	Late Famennian	*Sinostega*	Early tetrapod
Central Belgium	Late Famennian	Strud jaw**	Early tetrapod
Tula region of Russia	Famennian	*Tulerpeton*	Early tetrapod
Western Latvia	Late Famennian	*Ventastega*	Early tetrapod

*Devonian Period
The Middle Devonian Epoch is divided into two stages:
    Eifelian (397.5 million to 391.8 million years ago)
    Givetian 391.8 million to 385.3 million years ago)
The Late Devonian Epoch is divided into two stages:
    Frasnian (385 million to 374 million years ago)
    Famennian (374 million to 359 million years ago)
**The "Strud jaw" is a lower-jaw fragment discovered at Strud in 1888 that measures about 7 cm in length and that represents the earliest known Late Devonian tetrapod from western continental Europe.

of amphibians. The story of land vertebrates was barely underway, however; soon, these animals would experience even greater diversification. This diversification eventually would lead to the evolution

(continues on page 116)

THINK ABOUT IT

How to Find a Late Devonian Tetrapod

Discovering a fossil specimen of a tetrapod from the Late Devonian Epoch is not a matter of chance. Evidence representing this critical stage in the transition of vertebrates from water to land is rare, and most of it is found in far-flung locations. A survey of the 13 fossil sites currently known to contain tetrapods from the Late Devonian reveals that more than half of the 16 recognized genera of such animals are known from scant evidence consisting of little more than a single skeletal element such as a jaw or limb bone. The sites are scattered around the world, mostly in remote locations in the Northern Hemisphere. In other words, Late Devonian fossil sites are scarce and, with only a few exceptions, difficult to get to. These logistical issues complicate exploration for early tetrapod fossils.

Many paleontologists hoping to find tetrapods have returned to well-established fossil deposits such as those in eastern Greenland. A more risky and daring strategy is to find a site that has never yielded tetrapods or near-tetrapods before. Ted Daeschler and Neil Shubin took the latter approach when they decided to explore Late Devonian geological formations in Nunavut, Canada, that had formed in shallow-water habitats that could have been exploited by early, transitional fish-tetrapods. Their gamble paid off with the discovery of *Tiktaalik*, a lobe-finned fish that probably lived in the water but whose anatomical features would have allowed it to crawl onto land from time to time.

The recognition of *Tiktaalik* was preceded by four years of exploring for fossils in the Canadian Arctic, where the summers are short and the sun shines for nearly 24 hours a day. The *Tiktaalik* site is located in a valley of the remote Ellesmere Island, about 600 miles north of the Arctic Circle in the Nunavut Territory. The expeditions have each included between six and eight scientists and students.

In 2000, tantalizing fossil fragments found at the site gave the scientists hope that they might be onto something related to the fish-tetrapod transition. It became clear to them that the site had once been subtropical

Tiktaalik was discovered in the Canadian Arctic, where the season for digging fossils is short because of cold weather.

in climate. It consisted of shallow-water stream deposits—an ideal habitat for the first tetrapods. Daeschler, Shubin, and other team members returned to the site several times, continuing their search until, in 2004, they recovered several well-preserved specimens of *Tiktaalik*. The fossils were collected while still mostly encased in rocks and were protected by plaster jackets. The protected fossils then were lifted by helicopter out of the site to begin their 3,000-mile journey back to the United States for complete preparation and study. Once research has been completed, the specimens will be returned to a Canadian scientific institution for permanent keeping.

What the team found after studying the fossil-bearing rocks was startling. No less than three partial specimens of *Tiktaalik* eventually emerged

(continues)

(continued)

as laboratory preparators carefully cleared away the rock matrix from the bones. Nearly two years later, a clear picture of *Tiktaalik* took shape, and Daeschler, Shubin, and their colleague Farish Jenkins published the details of their discovery in the journal *Nature* in April 2006.

What, you may ask, is the significance of the discovery's name? The scientists borrowed the name *Tiktaalik* from the language of the residents in the region of the Canadian Arctic where the fossil was found. The name, which is pronounced tick-TAH-lick, is an Inuktikuk word for a large, shallow-water fish.

(continued from page 113)

of reptiles and mammals, two groups that, in turn, would make themselves masters over the great variety of life-forms.

DIVERSIFICATION OF EARLY TETRAPODS: THE CARBONIFEROUS AND PERMIAN PERIODS

The beginning of the Carboniferous Period, 360 million years ago, was a time of expanding horizons for all terrestrial life. Plants were extending their domain in all directions, gaining ground and pushing out farther from the shorelines of the oceans, lakes, and streams where they originated. Insects and other arthropods were thriving in the vast vegetative coal forests that accumulated around the coastal plains. The annual climate was so evenly temperate that there were no distinct seasons. Tree rings, which are caused by pauses in seasonal growth, are absent from fossil trees from the Middle Carboniferous.

Into the humid, swampy habitats of the Carboniferous walked a variety of early tetrapods, the first amphibians. Because the fossil record for early tetrapods is spotty going into the Carboniferous, the roots and connections for many tetrapods known from this period are unclear. Even so, the variety and diversity of Carboniferous tetrapods is hard to deny, and their success is marked by an apparent radiation into several ecological niches, where they immediately dominated as top predators. In geologic terms, their reign would be short, however; it was curbed by the rise of early amniotes (reptiles) in particular during the beginning of the Permian. The legacy of these early tetrapods survives today in the taxonomic group Lissamphibia: modern-day amphibians, including frogs, toads, salamanders, and caecilians. Following are representative families and members of the early tetrapods.

Crassigyrinidae (Early Carboniferous). *Enigmatic* and *peculiar* are words often used to describe the lone member of this **clade**, *Crassigyrinus*, whose names means "shallow wriggler." Found only in Scotland and known from three skulls and a nearly complete skeleton, *Crassigyrinus* was about 6.5 feet (2 m) long, with extremely short limbs, a long, finlike tail, and a large skull that alone measured about 14 inches (35 cm) long. This puzzling, eel-like creature with tiny legs seems more like a fish than a tetrapod, yet characteristics of its skeleton and limbs clearly show that its most immediate ancestors were fully limbed amphibians. *Crassigyrinus* apparently evolved from a lineage of tetrapods that after many generations on land actually returned to specialize for life in the water, making it secondarily aquatic from the standpoint of its evolution. Evolution does not always go in one direction.

Whatcheeriidae (Early Carboniferous). This recently discovered family of tetrapods includes two genera, each measuring about 3.5 feet (1 m) long. *Pederpes*, from Scotland, was described by Jennifer Clack in 2002 based on a nearly complete skeleton held in the collections of the Hunterian Museum, Glasgow, since 1971. Although originally it was misidentified as a fish, further preparatory work on the specimen nearly 30 years later revealed that it had legs. Clack immediately recognized a significant new twist in the orientation of the legs of *Pederpes* when the specimen was compared to other Late Devonian tetrapods. Instead of having bony fins pointed backwards, up, or to the sides for paddling, *Pederpes* had limbs that were oriented so that the animal could swing its feet forward for walking. "The locomotion of *Pederpes* is quite different to what went before," notes Clack, explaining that later tetrapods continued to improve on this forward-swinging bone configuration. Equipped with five functional digits on its forelimbs and feet, *Pederpes* is the earliest known tetrapod to depart from the fin and paddle design of Late Devonian tetrapods. This makes *Pederpes* the earliest known vertebrate equipped primarily for terrestrial locomotion.

Even though *Pederpes* might also have had a sixth tiny finger on its forelimb, it appears that the whatcheeriids were beginning to settle on five digits as the optimal number for walking on land—a pattern that would stick in most other lines of tetrapods throughout the Carboniferous and beyond. *Pederpes* and its slightly younger relative Whatcheeria (discovered in 1995 in Iowa) are the best-known tetrapods marking the early part of the Carboniferous Period.

Baphetidae (Carboniferous). This tetrapod group is known mainly from the skulls of four genera; little is known about their postcranial remains. The skulls were broad and flat and shaped somewhat like the head of a shovel when viewed from above. The jaws were lined with rows of pointed teeth, suggesting a diet of fish. The roof of the mouth was fitted with additional, longer, fanglike teeth in some genera, such as *Megalocephalus*. The skull openings for the eyes of the baphetids were somewhat irregular and shaped almost like keyholes, with an extension of the orbit just in front of where the eye would have been. This additional surface may have been a place for the attachment of powerful jaw muscles.

Aside from the shared similarity of the elongated eye sockets, the known baphetids differed in many ways. The most elongate skull of the group, measuring up to 14 inches (36 cm), was that of *Megalocephalus* (Scotland, England, Ireland); this skull had a crocodilelike appearance. *Spathicephalus* (Nova Scotia, England) had a rounder, flatter skull, with its eyes positioned close together on either side of the midline of the top of the skull. *Loxomma* (Scotland) had a blunt

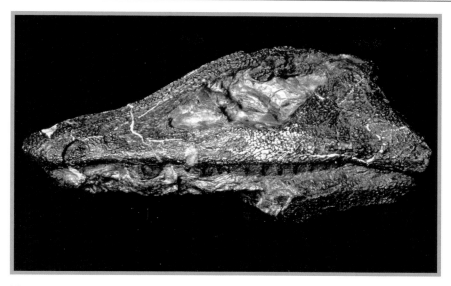

Megalocephalus had a blunt snout, flattened skull, and eyes that protruded out of the water while the animal was submerged.

snout, a flattened skull, and eyes that protruded out of the water while the animal was submerged. *Baphetes* (England) had a slightly elongate, shovel-shaped skull measuring 11 inches (29 cm) long.

Colosteidae (Carboniferous). The colosteids are one of the best-known tetrapod groups from the Early Carboniferous. They included medium-sized amphibians with salamanderlike bodies. Growing up to four feet (1.5 m) long, the colosteids had short legs and long, low, and flat skulls. They probably were largely aquatic, feeding on fish. The colosteid skull was somewhat like that of *Acanthostega*. A distinctive feature was a pair of tusklike teeth located in the front upper jaw. These tusks were accommodated by a notch in the lower jaw. Colosteids might represent an early branch of the primitive amphibians, also known as temnospondyls. Notable genera of colosteids include *Greererpeton* and *Colosteus* from North America.

Dendrerpeton (Late Carboniferous). The genus *Dendrerpeton* (Late Carboniferous, Nova Scotia) was a basal amphibian and one of the earliest to show strong affinities for life on land. It had strong limbs and sturdy hip and shoulder girdles and was about 40 inches (100 cm) long. The stapes bone in *Dendrerpeton*'s skull was oversized; it probably was used for structural support rather than for hearing, but the presence of this bone is an important link to later tetrapods in which the stapes became part of the ear. Specimens of *Dendrerpeton* are often found inside fossilized tree trunks; this attests to its terrestrial habitation.

Aïstopoda (Early Carboniferous to Early Permian). This small group of legless amphibians is classified with the tetrapods. Despite the fact that aïstopods had no limbs, traits such as the structure of the backbone shared affinities with other groups of tetrapods. Snakelike in appearance, aïstopods evolved long before the first snakes and were unrelated; however, the aïstopods may have filled an ecological niche similar to that of snakes. It is presumed that the ancestors of aïstopods had limbs and made the curious adaptation of a legless condition for whatever advantages it provided this line of tetrapods. The aïstopods grew up to three feet (100 cm) long. *Lethiscus* and other members of this taxon illustrate the great diversity of the Carboniferous radiation of amphibians and their adaptations to a variety of lifestyles.

Anthracosauria (Early Carboniferous to Early Triassic). This group includes several small- to medium-sized reptilelike amphibians that are thought to be more closely related to amniotes than to other early amphibian lines. The bodies of these animals were generally long; some forms were more terrestrial than others. The skulls retained some of the weaker, less fused structural features of lobe-finned fishes. *Proterogyrinus* (Early Carboniferous, West Virginia, Scotland) had a long, scooping mouth lined with small, pointed teeth for snatching fish. Its vertebral column, ribs, and limbs were more than adequate for trekking on land, but *Proterogyrinus* also retained a tall, flat-sided tail that would have enabled it to swim effectively. *Pholiderpeton* (Late Carboniferous, England) appeared to be at home in the water. It had short limbs; a broad, flat tail; a short neck; and an elongate, crocodilelike body.

Nectridea (Late Carboniferous to Permian). The Late Carboniferous and Early Permian Periods marked the height of amphibian diversity and dominance of world terrestrial habitats. Amphibian tetrapods had expanded in many directions at once, using a diversity of body forms, although most still were dependent on being near water to breed. While many taxa became increasingly adapted for the land, some tetrapods found great success by remaining mostly aquatic. The nectrideans were among those. *Sauropleura* (Late Carboniferous, Europe and North America) was among the more salamanderlike forms of nectrideans; it had a long, flattened tail for swimming. The vertebrae of the *Sauropleura* tail were unique among early tetrapods: These vertebrae had large, symmetrically designed bony elements above and below the hollow channel that housed the **notochord**. Clearly distinguishing *Sauropleura* from present-day salamanders were the presence of rows of sharp, pointed teeth in the upper and lower jaws.

Among the best-known nectrideans is *Diplocaulus* (Late Carboniferous and Early Permian, Texas). Remains of these animals that represent several growth stages have been found. Measuring about three feet (1 m) long, *Diplocaulus* had body protuberances on either side of its flat skull; this gave it a decidedly boomerang-shaped head. The body was broad but flat. One can imagine this robust predator resting quietly on the bottom of a stream, holding its breath and waiting for prey to swim above. *Diplocaulus* had a relatively short tail for an aquatic tetrapod; five toes on each fore-limb and hind limb; a wide, gaping mouth; anteriorly positioned nostrils; and eyes that faced upward. The animal's boomerang skull was nearly as wide as the trunk of its body was long. The unusually shaped skull probably aided the bulky swimmer as it glided through the water, providing lift much as an airplane wing does. The wide skull with its pointed wings would have been difficult for a predator to swallow. This probably discouraged some potential attackers from snapping at the head of *Diplocaulus*, although the trunk of its body was certainly vulnerable and would have made a substantive meal without the head.

Eryopoidea (Permian). This was once a group containing many forms of early amphibians that had been difficult to place anywhere else in the lineage of early tetrapods, but the eryopids have since been reduced by further study to two families based on the bony structure of their nasal passages and hips. While most members of these families appear to have been largely aquatic, the best-known genus is the large, terrestrial animal known as *Eryops* (Early Permian, United States). *Eryops* was large. It measured up to eight feet (2.5 m) long and could crawl with relative ease across the fallen trees and swampy terrain of its habitat. Fossils of *Eryops* were common enough that for many years it was the most featured early amphibian in the world's leading natural history museums, forming a picture of the first tetrapods as large, hulking brutes. Recent discoveries, many of which are outlined in these pages, now provide a more complete picture of early tetrapod design and make *Eryops*, with its massive limbs and skeleton, less typical of the amphibians that dominated the Late Paleozoic Era.

Seymouriamorpha (Permian). This taxon and its best-known member, *Seymouria* (Late Permian, Texas), includes the most reptilelike of the early tetrapods. The affinities of the group with the first reptiles—the first amniotes—include legs that are more robust and locomotive than those of most early tetrapods and a vertebrae design that anticipates that seen in amniotes, which also were appearing during the same time span. The skull was taller than that of most early amphibians, and the upper jaw was equipped with fanglike teeth. *Seymouria* has been known since the 1880s, and most paleontologists considered it to be an early reptile until more recent studies began to reveal more and more affinities with amphibians. The study of growth-series specimens in the mid-1990s showed that seymouriamorphs had an early aquatic stage with gills before they grew into their terrestrial form. This clearly marks *Seymouria* and its kin as amphibians. Nonetheless, *Seymouria* was one of the best adapted of the early terrestrial amphibians, and at a length of about 23 inches (60 cm) long, it probably was a fit competitor of the first reptiles.

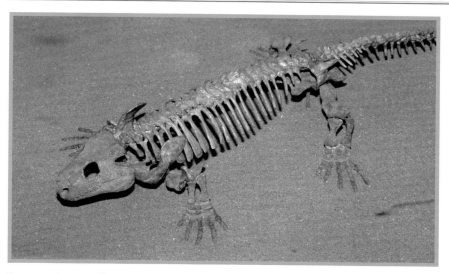

Seymouria was the most reptilelike of the early tetrapods.

COMPETITION

As the dominant tetrapods of the Carboniferous Period, amphibians reigned as top predators in many niches for 70 million years or more. This reign may have been limited, however, by the amphibians' dependency on breeding in the water. This reliance kept most amphibian lineages close to the water and inhibited their expansion beyond the horizon, where drier, more temperate habitats provided additional ecological opportunities.

The vertebrates that first broke away from a life bound to the water were the amniotes—animals that produced eggs with a protective outer membrane, a development that made it possible to breed out of the water. Modern amniotes include reptiles, mammals, and birds. The roots of all amniote lineages go back to the Late Carboniferous Period and the evolution of the first reptiles. The origins and diversification of the first amniotes is the subject of Chapter 6.

SUMMARY

This chapter described the first animals to make the transition from water to land and explored the great diversity of early tetrapods.

1. Two overlapping evolutionary stages in the Devonian history of tetrapod origins included the development of near-tetrapod sarcopterygians and near-terrestrial tetrapods.

2. The earliest traces of tetrapods come in the form of partial body fossils and trackways that date from the latter part of the Devonian, about 370 million to 380 million years ago.

3. Of the lobe-finned fishes, the group known as the osteolepiforms includes the most likely evolutionary precursors of the first limbed vertebrates.

4. Near-terrestrial tetrapods represent an important transitional stage in the evolution of limbed vertebrates but also appear better suited for life in shallow waters. *Acanthostega*, a water-bound tetrapod, provides fossil evidence that limbs developed for use in the water prior to tetrapods' taking to land.

5. Early tetrapods greatly diversified during the Carboniferous and Permian Periods. They were the top land predators of the Carboniferous, occupying many habitats with a variety of body forms and sizes, including legless and aquatic families that had returned full time to the water.

6. Amphibians were displaced as the top land predators during the Permian Period with the spread of the first amniotes, the reptiles.

SECTION THREE:
THE EVOLUTION
OF EARLY AMNIOTES

TAKING OVER THE LAND: REPTILES AND THEIR KIN

The journey of the tetrapods began with the appearance of limbs to help them move about and ambush prey more readily while still living a waterborne life. From the shallow lakes and streams of Carboniferous forests emerged a variety of amphibians ready to divide their time between life on the land and life in the water—an environment to which it was still necessary to go to breed. The next big leap in the history of tetrapods began about 310 million years ago, in the Late Carboniferous, when a group of small-sized creatures developed adaptations that increasingly distanced them from their ancestral dependency on water for breeding. This latter line of vertebrates was the group known as the amniotes, and it was their new reproductive strategy that would soon place them atop the food chain as the most formidable predators of their age.

AMNIOTE ORIGINS

Prior to the appearance of amniotes, all tetrapods reproduced in the water. With most extant amphibians, fertilization takes place externally; the same can be assumed for the earliest tetrapods. Typically, when two amphibians mate underwater, the male discharges sperm onto mature eggs that are being released from the body of the female. The egg mass is covered in a gelatinous substance; this sticky substance adheres the eggs to a surface such as a rock. Soon, an aquatic larva hatches from each egg. It swims freely, breathes through gills, eats food, and grows rapidly. The larva undergoes

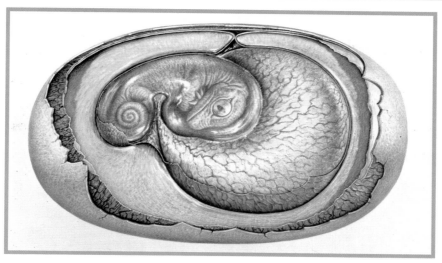

An amniotic egg protects the embryo within the sealed environment of an egg that can be laid out of the water. The egg is also a self-sufficient environment, needing only oxygen from the outside.

metamorphosis during which it grows limbs, develops lungs, and leaves the water as an air-breathing creature.

Reptiles and later tetrapods are considered more advanced than amphibians partly because of their reproductive strategy. This reproductive strategy is at the heart of being a reptile, a mammal, or a bird—a commonality that unites these vertebrates into a group known as the **Amniota**. An amniote protects the embryo of its offspring within the sealed environment of an amniotic egg. The egg is more or less impervious and protects the embryo from the outside environment. The egg is also a self-sufficient environment, needing only oxygen from the outside. The term amniote is derived from the word *amnion*, the name for a membrane that forms a fluid-filled sac around the embryo in the eggs of reptiles, mammals, and birds.

All extant amniotes are derived from the first such animals, the earliest reptiles, that arose during the Late Carboniferous Period. The early reptiles, like most of their living descendants, including birds, evolved a shelled egg that could be left exposed to the air in a dry environment. Amniotes also include the mammals and some kinds of reptiles that give birth to live young but retain the same general pattern of egg and embryo development inside the body of the mother.

The first reptiles succeeded by breeding out of the water, exploring new habitats and extending their ecological and geographic range. Just how the first egg-laying reptiles evolved is a paleontological puzzle with little hard evidence but an extremely sensible theory. Alfred Romer once summed up the entire tale by concluding that, "It was the egg that came ashore first before the adult was ready to follow it." This statement at first seems to be disconnected from reality, as it seems to imply that reptiles would lay eggs on land without being ready to live on land. In view of the fact that many of the tetrapods of the Middle Carboniferous were still semiaquatic, one of the last vestiges of their water-bound life would certainly have been their practice of breeding in the water. The behavior associated with reproduction, however, is not entirely driven by an organism's genetic signals. Reproduction is also strongly influenced by environmental factors. Those factors can favor an organism with a slightly different reproductive strategy that gives its offspring a better chance for survival. Romer speculated that the lakes and streams of the Carboniferous were teeming with fishes, arthropods, and aquatic tetrapods, all anxiously tracking down their next meal. This belief is supported by the rich fossil record of aquatic life from the time. Even today, amphibian eggs, once hatched into tadpoles, provide an abundant food source for other aquatic creatures. To compensate for the guaranteed loss of most of their young, amphibians lay an enormous number of eggs to increase the odds of continuing their kind. It is not unusual for a species of frog or toad to lay several hundred eggs in a single mass. The northern leopard frog and eastern American toad vastly exceed the norm by laying between 4,000 and 8,000 eggs at one time.

It would appear that some early tetrapods took the protective step of laying their eggs on land. Just how a gelatinous egg mass could survive out of the water does not require too much imagination.

In a rain-forest habitat such as that seen in many Carboniferous terrestrial ecosystems, there would have been many damp, moist, continually wet places under logs, beneath ground-covering plants, in tree stumps, and in other shaded places where amphibians could deposit their eggs and breed. In fact, there are many species of frogs and salamanders today that do just that. Laying jelly-covered eggs in a moist, protected spot on land may have been the first step in the evolution of amniotes. Over time, the designs of eggs laid on land were selected to favor those that began to develop special membranes, including a hard outer shell that protected the embryo but also permitted gas exchange to let oxygen inside.

The transition from breeding in the water to laying eggs on land necessitated leaving behind the waterborne tadpole, the larval stage of growth. How this transition was made is unknown from the fossil record. An intermediate step toward fully terrestrial hatchlings might have resembled the manner in which several species of frogs care for their larval young today. Instead of letting their tadpoles swim freely in open water, some frogs have developed special pouches on their bodies in which they carry the tadpoles until the young metamorphose into their terrestrial form. Perhaps some early amphibians had a similar practice while making the transition to land, possibly skipping the tadpole stage entirely, with hatchlings born as immature but wholly formed imitations of the adults.

The first reptiles were tiny in comparison to the hulking amphibians that dominated the swamps of the Carboniferous. Their small size is probably related to the development of the amniotic egg. By skipping the tadpole stage, reptiles lost an opportunity to grow larger before becoming acclimated to life outside the water. This possibly explains why the first known reptiles measured only a few inches long: Skipping the tadpole stage made for smaller individuals. Small size was not a trait that would characterize reptiles for long, however. By the Permian Period, as amniotes diversified, so, too, did they grow larger and more dominant in whatever habitat they occupied.

REPTILES: THE FIRST AMNIOTES

The earliest reptile for which there is clear, undisputed fossil evidence is *Hylonomus,* from the Middle Carboniferous swamps of Nova Scotia; it dates from about 310 million years ago. Another early reptile, *Paleothyris*, dates from about 300 million years ago and also comes from Nova Scotia. Superb fossils of each have been found inside fossilized tree trunks. It is presumed that the animals perished inside the exposed tree trunks while feeding on insects, millipedes, and other arthropods that may have lived there. The reptiles may have drowned or been buried by sediment during a significant flood event. Their bodies, buried in mud and sand, were eventually fossilized as the mud and sand turned to stone.

Hylonomus and *Paleothyris* represent the kind of small, lightly built tetrapods that one might expect from animals that were breaking the evolutionary link to water and hatching from eggs on dry land. The two animals show several key anatomical traits in transition from the forms of their amphibious ancestors.

Of particular importance were the skull designs of *Hylonomus* and *Paleothyris*, which diverged significantly from those of early amphibians. Amphibians such as *Ichthyostega* had large, flat, crocodile-shaped skulls with wide mouths. Such mouths were powered by a suite of strong but simple muscles at the rear of the skull. *Ichthyostega* and similar taxa were adept at snapping their mouths closed on prey, but they could not tighten the grip because their jaws were not designed to be squeezed tight. Their teeth functioned as little more than grappling hooks, snagging prey and trapping it in the huge mouth cavity. This design worked well for a diet that probably consisted largely of fish and other soft, waterborne creatures. But it did not enable the first amphibians to take much advantage of the vast, untapped terrestrial food sources represented by hard-bodied arthropods and plants.

Hylonomus and *Paleothyris* show adaptations in jaw design that allowed them to capitalize on land-based food sources. Their skulls were smaller, sturdier, and taller than those of early amphibians, and their jaws were lined with an impressive battery of small, pointed

Hylonomus was one of the earliest reptiles to make a clean break from life in the water.

teeth. Unlike the jaw muscles of *Ichthyostega*, the jaw muscles of *Hylonomus* and *Paleothyris* were larger in proportion to the size of their skulls and connected in two different arrays. In *Hylonomus* and *Paleothyris*, one set of muscles provided the snapping action for grabbing prey, and the other set of muscles provided strength for pressing the jaws together to maintain grip. The taller skull, smaller jaw, and larger muscles also provided more leverage so that these early reptiles could hold tightly to prey that could not initially be trapped inside the mouth.

Plants represented a widely abundant new source of food for vertebrates. The earliest fossil evidence for plant-eating animals comes from petrified excrement from the Late Silurian Period.

Although the identity of these animals cannot be known, their fossilized feces—known as **coprolites**—contain tiny bits of plant material and spores. By the Permian Period, reptiles in significant numbers had adapted to eating vegetation. Their strong jaws and squeezing bite proved effective in gnawing and chewing the seedless vascular plants and gymnosperms that were plentiful in the coal forests of tropical zones. The development of large-scale herbivory began a new stage in the interrelationships of plants and animals and affected the evolutionary development of all organisms in the ecosystem. As plant eaters grew and diversified, so, too, did the predatory traits of the meat eaters who fed on them. Plants also adapted protective measures against herbivores; this resulted in a variety of tough outer skins, spines, and tougher leaves to serve as defensive measures.

The skull design of early reptiles evolved ways to make the action of the jaws increasingly effective. By the Late Carboniferous Period, reptiles began to develop small openings in the skull behind the eye socket. This window in the skull provided additional space for the attachment of muscles while maintaining a strong but lightweight skull design that allowed these tetrapods to remain quick and agile even as they diversified into larger forms.

Evolution of the Tetrapod Vertebral Column

Some of the most important clues to the lineage of early tetrapods can be traced in the evolutions of the vertebral column. While all vertebrates have a backbone, the number of vertebrae and the shape and design of the individual bones vary significantly from taxon to taxon. Such morphological features as size, shape, and volume provide excellent clues to the lifestyle of a given extinct creature. The design of vertebrae can also serve as pointers to link related taxa.

To understand the vertebral column, one must first understand the language used to describe the individual components of the backbone. The fundamental purpose of the backbone is to protect the spinal cord and notochord and to provide a supportive frame for an animal. A single vertebra (plural: vertebrae) consists of two basic parts. The centrum (plural: centra) is the central part of the bone, through which the notochord runs; the centrum provides a resting place for the spinal cord. On top of the centrum is the neural arch, which rests on top of the spinal cord. In addition, a variety of riblike structures may also be present, depending on the kind of animal. Ribs along the trunk of the animal may be joined to the vertebrae at both the centra and the neural arches. A tail vertebra may have another extension called the haemal arch joined to the underside of the centrum.

The designs of centra and arches sometimes provide distinguishing feature of individual vertebrate taxa. Along with clues in the skull, the limbs, and the pectoral and pelvic girdles, these clues in the bones tell much of the story of how the animal lived and what other creatures it was related to. The vertebral column governs an animal's structural posture, mobility, and flexibility. In the continuing story of the prehistoric Earth, the vertebral column will join the skull, jaws, teeth, and limb elements as a key tool to use in diagnosing the evolutionary relationship of extinct groups.

The design of the backbone of the first reptiles provided support as well as lightness and flexibility; this differed in significant ways from the skeletal features of lumbering amphibians from the same time. The lifestyle of swamp-bound amphibians was not demanding when it came to hunting prey. *Acanthostega* and *Ichthyostega* probably rested quietly in pools of shallow water, waiting for unwary fish to swim close enough to be snapped up and gobbled down.

Land-based prey in the Carboniferous included arthropods, such as insects, and tetrapods. Reptiles undoubtedly required a more mobile lifestyle than that of amphibians if the reptiles were to catch such prey. The lightly built backbones of reptiles provided structural strength and flexibility of movement. The cervical, or neck, vertebrae were highly modified over those of the reptiles' amphibian ancestors and included a ball-and-socket connection with the skull. This flexible neck allowed the head to rotate, an advantage when catching prey as well as a means of providing improved flexibility while the animal was walking and running.

The vertebral columns of these early reptiles also provided increasingly strong attachments to the forelimbs and hind limbs of the animals. Although the length of their legs was not yet significantly different from that of their amphibian precursors, the earliest reptiles were the first tetrapods to show an important modification to the ankle bones. Basal amphibian ankles were made up of many small bones that provided improved flex over the fins of fish; this made walking on land more feasible. Reptiles such as *Hylonomus* and *Paleothyris* showed an additional improvement by fusing three of the ankle bones into a single unit called the *astragalus*. This change provided a better orientation of the foot for walking on land.

PRELUDE TO DIVERSIFICATION

By the end of the Carboniferous Period, the amniote solution for reproducing on land began to pay dividends. Fully terrestrial land vertebrates were diversifying rapidly and taking advantage of the seemingly unlimited opportunities of greening habitats and generous food supplies. Reptiles began to diversify, leaving fossil evidence of 25 or more taxa of such insect-eating and plant-eating creatures. Most were small, like *Hylonomus* and *Paleothyris*, measuring about eight inches (20 cm) long; however, larger taxa were beginning to appear.

As reptiles diversified into many ecological niches, they began new branches of the vertebrate family tree. *Hylonomus* and *Paleothyris,* the most basal reptiles, represent the first radiation of these animals. Going into the Permian Period, the lineage of terrestrial vertebrates exploded in several directions that eventually led to the rise of dinosaurs, other reptile groups, birds, and mammals. The Permian Period introduces these new forms of vertebrates and their evolutionary foundation they provided for the Mesozoic Era—the Age of Reptiles.

SUMMARY

This chapter introduced the first amniotes and described the adaptations that led to their dominance of terrestrial environments by the time of the Permian Period.

1. Prior to the appearance of amniotes, all tetrapods reproduced in the water.

2. An amniote protects the embryo of its offspring within the sealed environment of an amniotic egg. Amniotes include all reptiles, mammals, and birds, but do not include fish and amphibians.

3. The amniote reproductive strategy eliminated the need for tetrapods to return to the water to breed, an important part of making them fully terrestrial.

4. The earliest known reptile is *Hylonomus*, from the Middle Carboniferous of Nova Scotia; it dates from about 310 million years ago.

5. Early amniote jaws were an improvement over early amphibian jaws, providing a stronger bite and the ability to squeeze the teeth together to cope more effectively with hard-bodied prey such as insects.

6. The design of the backbone of the first reptiles provided support as well as lightness and flexibility, differing in significant ways from the skeletal features of amphibians from the same time.

7. Early reptiles had stronger ankle bones that also provided better orientation of the foot for walking on land.

7

VERTEBRATES BRANCH OUT

By about 299 million years ago, at the beginning of the Permian Period, basal amniotes had already begun to show adaptations leading to their branching into four distinct clades of amniotes. The distinguishing features of these four groups are many, but they begin with a simple distinction in the design of the animals' skulls. From these four groups arose all of the terrestrial vertebrate families known today. This chapter reviews the rise of the four main groups of amniotic vertebrates that closed the Paleozoic Era and led to the rise of reptiles as the dominant life-form of the Mesozoic Era.

SPLITS IN THE AMNIOTE FAMILY TREE

Several patterns of distinctive morphological changes began to arise in amniotes in the Carboniferous Period. These changes were most clearly expressed in the skulls of early reptiles and their kin. By the end of the Permian Period, about 251 million years ago, the die was cast for the future of amniotes that have dominated terrestrial, and sometimes marine, ecosystems ever since.

A key diagnostic trait used to classify amniotes is a feature of the skull called the **temporal fenestrae**—openings or "windows" in the skull just behind the orbit on the side of the skull, or temple region. Prior to the appearance of temporal fenestrae, the skulls of amniotes had openings only for sense organs, including the eyes, the nostrils, and the pineal "eye," a sense organ on top of the reptilian brain that was light sensitive. There are two biological reasons for the development of the temporal fenestrae. The movement and strength of the jaws relies on the attachment of muscles near the back of the skull, and such fenestrae provide grips for muscles as well as space for them to expand and contract as the jaw moves. Land animals needed more jaw power than fishes to adapt to terrestrial food consumption. Having holes in the temple region of the skull provided space and attachment areas for larger, more complex groups of jaw muscles.

Another benefit of the temporal fenestrae is the reduction of the weight of the skull and, presumably, the conservation of the calcium used to build and maintain strong bones. As vertebrates grew larger over time, skull bones as well as other skeletal elements such as vertebrae would evolve additional innovative shapes, cavities, and fenestrae to provide strength while also lightening the load on the body. The evolution of the temporal fenestrae was an important step in vertebrate experiments to modify skeletal morphology to increase the efficiency of the organism.

The absence or presence of the temporal fenestrae attests to the reptilian origins of all amniotes. The earliest amniotes had no temporal fenestrae, a condition considered basal and close to their amphibian ancestry. For the purposes of classification, amniotes can be placed into one of the following four groups based on skull design. All four of these conditions had taken shape in various lines of amniotes by the end of the Paleozoic Era.

Anapsida: These are amniotes with no temporal fenestrae, including the earliest reptiles. This clade includes *Hylonomus* and *Paleothyris* and several other extinct Late Carboniferous reptiles as well as the living tortoises and turtles, which were only recently added based on molecular evidence connecting them to the anapsids. The first anapsids appeared in the Middle Carboniferous Period.

Synapsida: These are amniotes with one temporal fenestra positioned somewhat behind and below the orbit of each eye. This clade includes all mammals as well as extinct mammal-like reptiles. Synapsids first appeared in the Late Carboniferous Period.

Diapsida: These are amniotes with two temporal fenestrae, a lower one like the one seen in synapsids and one just above it and behind the orbit. Lizards, snakes, crocodiles, and birds are included in this group, as well as extinct dinosaurs and pterosaurs (flying reptiles). Diapsids first appeared in the Late Carboniferous Period.

Euryapsida: These are amniotes with one temporal fenestra positioned just above and behind the orbit. Extinct marine reptiles belonging to this group include nothosaurs, plesiosaurs, and ichthyosaurs, most of which thrived in the Mesozoic Era. Euryapsids probably evolved from diapsids with the loss of the lower fenestrae. Euryapsids first appeared in the Early Permian Period.

ANAPSIDA: TURTLES AND THEIR EXTINCT KIN

The earliest reptiles, including *Hylonomus* and *Paleothyris*, were small-sized insectivores that lived among the vegetative debris and tree stumps of the Middle Carboniferous forest. They are numbered among the first anapsids, the most ancient lineage of reptiles. *Hylonomus* and *Paleothyris* had a superficial resemblance to today's lizards, but they were not directly related to them. *Hylonomus* and *Paleothyris* were probably quick on their feet and well adapted for life on land.

Between the Late Carboniferous and the Early Permian, the anapsid reptiles diverged in several directions. One surprising development was a return to the water of a group of Southern Hemisphere anapsids known as mesosaurs. Measuring about 3.5 feet (1 m) long, the mesosaur body was long and reminiscent of that of a crocodile. The limbs of the mesosaurs retained the basic design of land-based tetrapods, but their digits were webbed to aid in swimming. The mesosaur tail was also modified for swimming: It had tall, flat sides down its length. Most curious was the long and narrow mesosaur jaw. The upper and lower jaws were lined with a mesh of needle-like teeth that the animal used to trap and filter small arthropods, fishes, and other swimming creatures out of the water.

In contrast to the small, lizardlike anapsids were the hulking pareiasaurs. Found only in rocks dating from the Late Permian, these animals were large, heavy creatures comparable in size to the hippopotamus. Measuring between 6 and 10 feet (1 and 3 m) long, pareiasaurs had powerful, stumplike limbs and a sturdy, humped back protected by armor studs. The skull was short and blunt, with an array of bony frills jutting out from the cheeks. This extraordinary armor plating suggests that pareiasaurs needed protection from some of the equally large predatory synapsid reptiles that shared their habitat.

Pareiasaurs had perfected the eating of plants through several adaptations to their skull and jaws. The pareiasaur skeleton shows evidence of a large hump over the neck, an indication of strong neck and jaw muscles. The blunt, serrated, leaf-shaped teeth of these animals clearly indicate that they fed on soft vegetation. The best-known pareiasaur is *Scutosaurus*—the "shield lizard"—from Late Permian deposits in western Russia. *Scutosaurus* measured about eight feet (2.4 m) long and had a height at the peak of the back of about six feet (1.8 m).

As successful as the anapsids were during the latter part of the Paleozoic Era, their longevity eventually would be whittled down to the survival of a scant few members. These survivors included the armor-plated turtles and tortoises, the earliest forms of which arose during the Late Triassic Period. A contributing factor in the demise of many anapsids probably was the rise of the synapsids, once known as mammal-like reptiles. The synapsids included among their members the largest predators of their time.

SYNAPSIDA: ANCESTRAL MAMMALS

Following closely on the appearance of the first anapsids was the rise of a group of reptiles that would one day lead to the development of all mammals—the Synapsida. True mammals did not appear until the Late Triassic Period, but evolutionary developments leading to them as a line of animals distinct from reptiles began as far back as the Early Permian.

Synapsids include two groups of animals. The pelycosaurs were large animals; they are first known from Late Carboniferous fossils. By the Late Permian, they were joined by a mixed group of predatory and herbivorous synapsids collectively known as therapsids. All of the synapsids were quadrupeds—four-footed animals.

Pelycosaurs: The Sailbacked Synapsids

The most familiar pelycosaurs are the sailbacked *Dimetrodon* and *Edaphosaurus*. Evolving during the Early Permian, each of these animals developed a large sail on its back; the sail was held upright by extremely elongated extensions of the neural arch of the back and tail bones. This large sail must have looked somewhat like a handheld fan, as it was covered by a membrane of vascularized skin—skin with blood vessels running through it. The function of the sail was probably to help regulate the body temperature of the animal. The sailbacked pelycosaur was most likely a cold-blooded, or **ectothermic,** creature; in the morning, it could warm itself more quickly than other animals by facing its sail toward the sun. Sunlight striking the sail would warm the blood circulating inside the sail membrane; that warmed blood then would circulate throughout the animal's body. This would have given the animal either a head start on catching prey or a jump start on escaping from a predator, whichever the case may have been.

Although having sails gave *Dimetrodon* and *Edaphosaurus* a similar appearance, they had very different lifestyles. Found in some productive fossil locations, including Texas, these two animals probably lived in the same habitat. Their interaction would have been strictly on an "as needed" basis, however, because *Dimetrodon* was a fierce predator and *Edaphosaurus* a plant eater.

Dimetrodon was about 11.5 feet (3.5 m) long, with a sail that reached a height of about five or six feet (1.5 to 1.8 m). It had a large, muscular head with powerful jaws. Its teeth were serrated for slicing flesh, much like a steak knife. In addition, *Dimetrodon* had longer teeth in the front of its jaws for stabbing its prey. It walked very much like a crocodile, with a sprawling gait and its belly barely off of the ground. Being cold-blooded, *Dimetrodon* probably could not run at top speed for more than a short time, so its hunting tactics likely consisted of chasing slower animals, ambushing others, and perhaps also eating carrion.

Edaphosaurus was a plant eater that also adapted a vascularized sail on its back for **thermoregulation**, or the control of body temperature. Its skull was much smaller in proportion to its body than that of *Dimetrodon*. The shallow jaws of *Edaphosaurus* were lined with uniformly sized, chisel-like teeth that the animal used to snip vegetation. The roof of the edaphosaur mouth contained a cluster of rounded, knoblike teeth for crushing plant matter taken into the mouth. *Edaphosaurus* grew up to ten feet (3 m) long and had a gait similar to that of *Dimetrodon*. Another distinguishing feature of *Edaphosaurus* was the design of its sail. Compared to the sail of *Dimetrodon*, that of *Edaphosaurus* had many small spines or articulations on the rays of its supporting sail bones. This may have increased the speed with which blood could have circulated through the sail. One can imagine that this would have allowed *Edaphosaurus* to warm up and get moving a little more quickly than *Dimetrodon*—an advantage that may have saved *Edaphosaurus* from its predatory neighbor on more than one occasion.

The pelycosaur line of synapsids was long lived but did not survive the mass extinction at the end of the Permian Period.

Therapsida

The therapsids arose during the Middle Permian, following the decline of the pelycosaurs. This diverse collection of later synapsids persisted until the Early Jurassic Epoch; the therapsids were displaced by diapsids, a group that included lizards and the early dinosaurs. With the therapsids, the elongated, sprawling body plan of the pelycosaurs gave way to the compact, sturdier build seen in many theraspids. A reduced tail and longer legs suggest that these animals were becoming better walkers than the belly-dragging pelycosaurs. The reduction of tail length also reduced the surface area of the skin; this eased the loss of body heat and allowed these animals to maintain a steadier body temperature. This move in the direction of **endothermy**—the state of being warm-blooded—was a significant innovation seen in true mammals.

Three important groups of therapsids were the dinoceplalids, the dicynodonts, and the cynodonts, Of these, only the latter two groups managed to survive the great Permian-Triassic mass extinction, one of the most devastating extinction events in the history of the Earth. If these two groups had not survived, the modern world would be inhabited by a different assemblage of creatures than is known today.

Dinocephalids: The "Terrible Heads"

There are about 40 genera of these carnivorous and herbivorous animals known from Late Permian fossil beds in Russia and South Africa. The name dinocephalids, or "terrible heads," describes these creatures' large heads, many of which were adorned with a variety of bony plates, horns, and jutting protuberances.

Titanophoneus and *Anteosaurus*, both from Russia, represent the successful predatory body plan of the dinocephalids. These two animals were stocky and heavily muscled, with deep, large skulls that measured about 24 inches (60 cm) long. Their front legs were longer and more sprawling than the hind limbs, which were more similar to the upright legs of later mammals. A distinctive feature of the dinocephalid predators was interlocking incisor (front) teeth and long, pointed canines that jutted from the front of the upper and lower jaws. These teeth interlocked and were visible outside the mouth when it was closed. Such teeth would have been effective at grabbing and clamping down on any size prey of the predator's choosing. *Titanophoneus* was more slender in build than *Anteosaurus*; *Titanophoneus* also retained a longer tail than other typical dinocephalids. These were large predators. Some specimens were up to 20 feet long (6 m) and in life probably weighed about 1,100 pounds (500 kg). This size is comparable to that of a modern-day rhinoceros.

Among the larger herbivorous dinocephalids was *Moschops*, also from Russia. This was another large and bulky animal, with a body plan similar to that of *Anteosaurus*. The head of *Moschops* was smaller, however, and its jaws were lined with peglike teeth designed to pick away at vegetation. *Moschops* was about 16 feet (4.8 m) long. Its skull was about four inches (10 cm) thick in places, suggesting that individual animals may have engaged in head-butting contests to win mates.

Dicynodonts: Widely Distributed Plant Eaters

Dicynodonts included about 70 known genera; they were the most populous herbivores of the Late Permian. The dicynodonts ranged in size from that of small rodents to specimens 10 feet (3 m) long. Most dicynodonts were wiped out by the end-Permian extinction, with the exception of some taxa that lasted through the Triassic Period.

The name *dicynodont* means "two dog teeth" and refers to the presence of two long tusks, or canines, in the upper front jaw of these animals. As formidable as these teeth may have appeared, the dicynodonts were actually plant eaters. Some dicynodonts, such as *Lystrosaurus*, had no teeth other than these canines. These animals used a sharp-edged beak to snip plants that were then ground to shreds against bony plates in the roof of the mouth.

Lystrosaurus was a medium-sized creature, only about three feet (1 m) long. Its body was stout, its legs were short and sprawled in the front, and it had a very short tail. The lifestyle of *Lystrosaurus* could be likened to that of a small hippopotamus: It waded through a swampy habitat, feeding on low-growing vegetation such as ferns and gymnosperms. *Lystrosaurus* capitalized on an uncomplicated formula for success, and it became one of the most widely distributed early amniotes. Its fossils have been found in China, Russia, South Africa, India, and even Antarctica. This distribution was used as biological evidence to support the tectonic plate movements that once connected these now widely separated landmasses.

The largest of the dicynodonts include specimens from the Middle to Late Triassic. *Placerias* is well known from the early part

The plant-eating dicynodont *Lystrosaurus* capitalized on a simple anatomical formula for success and became one of the most widely distributed early amniotes.

of the Late Triassic Epoch, a time when the first dinosaurs were emerging. *Placerias* was probably the largest herbivore in its habitat; it measured about 10 feet (3 m) long. *Placerias* was similar in appearance to *Lystrosaurus*, but the skull of *Placerias* was longer, and its neck was more developed. In the front of its jaws, *Placerias* had a more birdlike beak than *Lystrosaurus*; also, *Placerias*'s dual tusks hung down from the sides of its mouth.

Cynodonts: Links to the First True Mammals

The cynodonts ("dog teeth") were a group of small synapsids that grew more plentiful and specialized during the Triassic Period.

The cynodonts were most likely the ancestors of mammals and developed several key adaptations that affiliate them closely with the radiation of early mammals during the Mesozoic Era. The evolutionary transformation of synapsid reptiles to mammals is one of the clearest cases of transitional modifications in the fossil record of vertebrates.

Even early cynodonts such as the long-nosed *Procynosuchus* (Later Permian, southern Africa) had affinities with true mammals. In *Procynosuchus*, such features as an enlarged nasal passage; a small but increasingly complex mosaic of jaw muscles, teeth, and bone; a more flexible joint connecting the neck and spine; and other anatomical features gave this small animal a look reminiscent of a modern rodent. While the overall appearance of *Procynosuchus* is strikingly mammal-like, however, the story of the transition from reptiles to mammals is told most clearly by examining stages in the development of the jaws of these animals.

The mechanics of the cynodont jaw was a particularly important step in the direction of true mammal traits. During the early evolution of the synapsids, the lower jaw was composed of many different bones. Over time, especially in the cynodonts, some of these individual jawbones either diminished in size or were displaced entirely by one larger bone called the dentary. The consolidation of the lower jaw into one sturdy mass was accompanied by a great simplification of the muscles associated with jaw mechanics. Instead of having three separate and equally dominant muscle groups for the jaw, as did early synapsids, the cynodonts developed the more mammal-like trait of having two more massive muscles occupying more and more space within the back of the skull. These changes to the cynodonts' jaw design are significant because they provided these ancestors of mammals—and eventually mammals themselves—with an impressive suite of chewing adaptations. Whereas most reptiles can move their jaws only up and down, mammals are able to chew using a triangulation pattern; this is a key adaptation for the development of improved dentition for chewing meat or a wide variety of vegetation. This adaptation resulted in the diversification of cynodont herbivores and insect-eating carnivores with increasingly complex batteries of tiny teeth.

Another gradual but radical anatomical change to cynodont jaws resulted in the development in cynodonts of mammal-like hearing. In early synapsids such as *Dimetrodon*, the lower jaw consisted of numerous small bones at the rear of the skull that formed the jaw joint. The eardrum was behind the jaw. In the cynodont *Thrinaxodon*, a change can be seen in the arrangement of these smaller jawbones. As the dentary bone became larger, and some of the small bones at the back of the lower jaw formed a new type of jaw joint, several of the remaining bones became smaller and migrated toward the ear region. In the earliest mammals, the same small bones were present but were no longer associated with the jaw joint. Instead, they became part of the hearing mechanism.

Thermoregulation, the control of body temperature, was an additional challenge for land animals. Tetrapods need to attain a certain optimum body temperature before they can become fully active for walking, feeding, hunting, and other physical activities. Large synapsids such as the pelycosaurs and dicynodonts relied on large body size to slow the gain or loss of heat, but this large size also made them relatively slow moving. Smaller animals, such as the cynodonts, did not have this size advantage. Instead, cynodonts probably maintained their body heat by eating frequently and remaining active to burn calories. Paleontologist David Norman suggests that the improved jaw designs of cynodonts had an important role in maintaining their energy level. The development of chewing enabled them to digest food more rapidly. A gradual separation of the nasal passages from the mouth cavity in mammal-like reptiles also allowed them to eat and breathe at the same time. Norman suggests that the need "to breathe quickly and regularly would not have been so great if they had been low-energy animals."

Cynodonts were small; most measured 24 inches (60 cm) long or less. The Early Triassic taxon *Thrinaxodon* (South Africa, Antarctica) was about 17 inches (45 cm) long, including its catlike tail. *Thrinaxodon* serves as a good example of the changes that took place in the posture and gait of mammal-like reptiles. Whereas the pelycosaurs and other synapsid groups had a sprawling posture, *Thrinaxodon* developed a more efficient gait through modifications of the hip girdle and hind legs. The result was legs that could be brought closer to the body in a semierect posture. The anatomical changes needed to make this happen included modifications to the shape of the leg bones and modifications to the shape of the muscles that powered them.

Cynognathus was a doglike carnivore. At about 3.5 feet (1 m) long, it was one of the largest of the cynodonts. Evolving during the Middle Triassic Epoch, *Cynognathus* was undoubtedly a fierce predator, and it represented another important milestone in the evolution of true mammals. The jaw of *Cynognathus* included three tooth designs, each contributing to the capture and consumption of prey. *Cynognathus* has long canine teeth for stabbing prey; small, pointed incisors for gripping prey; and serrated cheek teeth for shredding the flesh of its victims. The dentary bone of *Cynognathus* was also a good example of the consolidation of the lower jawbones: Ninety percent of this animal's lower jaw was made up of this single bone.

An even more doglike cynodont was *Probelesodon,* from the Late Triassic of Argentina. Its limbs were more fully erect than those of earlier cynodonts and gave this dog-sized predator speed and maneuverability. Some fossil specimens of *Probelesodon* show tiny pits on the snout; this suggests that these animals had doglike whiskers. If this was the case, one might further speculate that these animals were fur covered, another adaptation seen in mammals that helps regulate body temperature.

DIAPSIDA: LIZARDS, SNAKES, CROCODILES, BIRDS, PTEROSAURS, DINOSAURS, AND EXTINCT KIN

The diapsids include the most diverse radiation of reptile forms. With roots going back to the Late Carboniferous Period, most Paleozoic diapsids were small, long-legged, swift-running forms that lived in the shadows—or ran away from the shadows, as the case may have been—of the much larger amphibians, anapsids, and synapsids that dominated the terrestrial ecosystems of the Permian. With the coming of the disastrous end-Permian mass extinction, the status of many life-forms was changed forever. That event led the once-lurking diapsids into position to prosper in the Mesozoic Era.

The success of the diapsids is demonstrated by their current numbers. There are about 14,600 species of living diapsids, including birds, crocodilians, lizards, and snakes. As impressive as these numbers are, the most dominant diapsids of all time are no longer with us: the dinosaurs, pterosaurs, mosasaurs, and their extinct ancestors that ruled various spans of the Mesozoic Era. Except for turtles, which are classed as anapsids, the diapsids represent all true reptiles currently known.

The diapsids are divided into two primary groups, the **Archosauria** and **Lepidosauria**. Each of these groups began to diversify and flourish early in the Triassic Period. These animals were preceded by a variety of diapsid lines that were mostly extinct by the end of the Triassic Period but that also figured importantly in the rise of diapsids as the dominant life forms of the Mesozoic.

Early Diapsids

The fossil record of Late Paleozoic diapsids is not complete enough to define their evolutionary relationships. Certain anatomical trends can be seen in their development, however, and that development became more and more specialized and advantageous as diapsids of various kinds diversified in the Triassic. Among these adaptations were long legs for running, long necks for added flexibility, lighter skulls, and the specialization of teeth for the consumption of both meat and plants.

One of the earliest known diapsid reptiles is *Petrolacosaurus,* from the Late Carboniferous of Kansas. This small creature measured a mere 15 inches (40 cm) long, including its tail. It featured a very slight skeleton and a tiny skull with a large orbit for its eyes—an indication of good eyesight. *Petrolacosaurus* also had long legs, another key difference between diapsids and other amniotes. Keen vision and speed made *Petrolacosaurus* well suited for giving chase to insects.

The evolutionary relationship between *Petrolacosaurus* and later diapsids from the Permian is unknown, but it is clear that by the turn of the Triassic Period, several unusual lines of diapsids had found some success living in the shadows of the larger, lumbering amphibians, anapsids, and synapsids of the time.

Coelurosauravus, from the Late Permian of Madagascar, was another small diapsid with a most unusual adaptation. It was one of the first known reptiles to develop a means for gliding through the air, a feature that is seen today in the flying dragon lizard of Southeast Asia. The ribs of *Coelurosauravus* were elongated out from its body to form a frame for a skin-covered gliding wing. This lightweight creature was about 16 inches (40 cm) long and had a "wingspan" of about 12 inches (30 cm). Although it was a glider and not a powered flier, *Coelurosauravus* demonstrated that diapsids were highly adaptable and explored a variety of niches, in this case living an elevated lifestyle out of the reach of large, ground-based predators.

Archosauria

The archosaurs, or "ruling reptiles," represent a formidable line of tetrapods that includes dinosaurs, pterosaurs, crocodiles, and birds. The archosaurs are distinguished from other diapsids by a number of anatomical features; these included an additional opening in the side of the skull, just in front of the orbit. Some lines of archosaurs also developed a more upright posture over time, with forelimbs and hind limbs positioned more squarely beneath the body. One of the first known archosaurs is *Protorosaurus,* from the Late Permian of Germany, a 6.5-foot (2 m) long reptile that was already beginning a trend for large size. *Protorosaurus* had a long neck, a long snout, and a narrow jaw filled with small, sharp teeth. In many respects, it resembled a prototype of the modern-day monitor lizard.

During the first half of the Triassic Period, archosaur predators grew larger, fiercer, and more widespread; they effectively took over the ecological niche left vacant by the synapsids at the end-Permian extinction. Archosaurian body plans diverged in many directions. The largest land predators included *Erythrosuchus* and its kin, from the Early Triassic of South Africa. These animals grew to 16 feet (5 m) long and were equipped with a deep, bulky head with massive jaws and bone-crushing teeth. Other archosaurian predators of the Early to Middle Triassic included the crocodilelike *Chasmatosuchus* (South Africa and Asia), which measured about 6.5 feet (2 m long).

Some archosaurs were plant eaters, and they, too, developed into fairly large animals by the Late Triassic.

As was the case with the early diapsids, archosaurian evolution is also known for some extraordinarily strange experiments. *Tanystropheus,* an archosaur from the Middle Triassic of Israel, Germany, and Switzerland, had a short body and a neck so long that it almost defies believability. The animal was about 10 feet (3 m) long, six feet (2 m) of which consisted of a long, stiff neck. The neck of *Tanystropheus* is itself a puzzle, as it is composed of only 10 elongated vertebrae. The mouth of *Tanystropheus* was equipped with small, carnivorous teeth. Many paleontologists assume that this animal lived in a near-shore environment, where it probably could take to the water to support its gawky body.

Another bizarre early archosaur is *Longisquama,* from the Early Triassic of Asia. This small creature measured only six inches (15 cm) long and was most akin to a lizard except for its unusual dorsal spines. Mounted on the back of *Longisquama* were a dozen or more stiff, bony frills arranged in a single row above the spine. They resembled a row of upright hockey sticks, and their purpose is not fully understood. The most likely explanation is that the frill row had no more function than that of display, either to ward off a predator, to attract a mate, or both. Some paleontologists have also suggested that these frills might have aided in heat exchange, could somehow have been used in gliding, or may have been some form of proto-feathers.

Another notably small archosaur was *Euparkeria,* a two-foot (60 cm) long creature found in Early Triassic rocks of South Africa.

Euparkeria was another important archosaur. Because it had hind legs that were one-third longer than its front legs, this tiny reptile could sometimes scamper on two feet—showing an early appearance of bipedalism.

With long and powerful hind legs, a strong neck, and a mouth full of recurved, biting teeth, *Euparkeria* had many affinities with the first dinosaurs that arose in the Late Triassic. Having hind legs that were one-third longer than its front legs suggests that this tiny powerhouse could sometimes scamper on two feet, an early appearance of bipedalism. This was another trait later perfected by its archosaurian relatives, the meat-eating dinosaurs.

The roots of the archosaurs, as represented by these earliest representatives, provided an evolutionary workshop for the spectacular rise of crocodiles, flying reptiles (pterosaurs), and dinosaurs, beginning in the Late Triassic Epoch.

Lepidosauria

Lizards, snakes, and two species of *Sphenodon*—the lizardlike tuatara of New Zealand—are the living descendants of the lepidosaurs, another early branch of the diapsid family tree. The earliest members of this group, the sphenodontians, appeared in the Late Triassic, grew diverse during the Jurassic Period, but then dwindled in numbers, probably due to increasing competition from lizards. The sphenodontian *Planocephalosaurus,* from the Late Triassic of England, was about eight inches (20 cm) long and appeared much like the living tuatara, but *Planocephalosaurus* has several anatomical features that distinguish it from lizards, including teeth that are fused to the jaw and cannot be replaced like the teeth of all other reptiles. The tuatara, like the living crocodile and the lobe-finned coelacanth fish, is in many ways a living fossil, having survived generation after generation, for millions of years, with very few evolutionary changes.

Latter forms of sphenodontians from the Mesozoic Era took a variety of novel forms, including one genus, *Pleurosaurus* of Germany, that become aquatic.

The most successful lepidosaurs emerged after the Triassic Period. The lizards arose during the Jurassic Period, and the snakes arose during the Cretaceous. Another extraordinary lepidosaur form, the mosasaurs, were fierce, fully aquatic predators that ruled the Late Cretaceous seas of North America and elsewhere. Some mosasaurs grew to over 49 feet (15 m) long.

EURYAPSIDA: EXTINCT MARINE REPTILES AND THEIR KIN

The roots of the euryapsid family tree are largely uncertain, although the design of the euryapsid skull, with its single temporal fenestra, looks very much like the skull of a diapsid without the lower opening. There is consensus among paleontologists that the euryapsid skull was probably a modification of the diapsid pattern.

Regardless of similarities in their skulls, most euryapsids arose during the Mesozoic as a diverse and plentiful group of reptiles that had returned to an aquatic lifestyle. Just as the dinosaurs conquered life on land, so, too, did the euryapsids become the dominant vertebrates in the oceans of the world. All of these marine reptiles remained air breathers but adapted paddlelike limbs and elongated and streamlined bodies that enabled them to swim well. Some developed needlelike teeth for snaring fish from the water, while others had teeth and bony chewing surfaces better suited for crushing hard-shelled crustaceans and other invertebrates.

Most of the euryapsids did not rise to prominence until the middle of the Mesozoic Era, an era beyond the timeframe discussed in *March Onto Land*. All four euryapsid groups are described here, however, with some additional notes on those members that could be found during the first half of the Triassic Period.

Placodontia (Early to Late Triassic): These early euryapsids were bottom-feeding reptiles that resembled armor-plated walruses. Of all the euryapsids, the placodonts were the least specialized for life in the water. The placodonts were small- to medium-sized creatures; most were only from 0.5 to 6.5 feet (0.15 to 2 m) long. These animals would have been dwarfed by other marine predators of the time. The placodonts' limbs were stumpy and not paddlelike; this design suggests that the animals stayed in shallow, near-shore waters and probably moved about by moving along clumsily on the sea floor.

Placodonts are rare in the fossil record. The first evidence of placodonts consisted of curious, black, rounded teeth that sometimes were discovered in limestone quarries in Germany during the nineteenth century. One collector, a man named Georg Münster (1776–1844) took an interest in these "beans," as the quarry diggers called them. In 1830, Münster expressed the opinion that these were teeth from ancient fishes. It was not until 1858 that the examination of a skull of one of these creatures revealed that it was a reptile and not a fish. The first placodonts to be described in great detail were *Placodus* ("flat tooth") and *Cyamodus* ("bean tooth"), in 1863.

Placodonts have been placed in two families based on the presence of body armor. The Placodontoidea, or unarmored placodonts, had only a hint of external body armor in the form of a bony knob on top of each vertebra. The Cyamodontoidea, or armored placodonts, developed a broad, turtlelike shell on their backs (the carapace); some forms had armor plating on the neck, skull, and tails as well.

Euryapsids arose during the Mesozoic as a diverse and plentiful group of reptiles that had returned to an aquatic lifestyle. Nothosaurs were long-necked marine reptiles with webbed feet or paddles. Placodonts had long stout bodies with armor plating and lived in near-shore environments.

Some members of the Cyamodontoidea also had an armor-plated underside similar to the plastron of turtles.

Placodus is the best-known member of the unarmored placodonts. It measured up to 6.5 feet (2 m) long and had a small head with strong jaws that seem to have been adapted for crushing hard-shelled mollusks. The front of the *Placodus* jaw had blunt, forward-pointing teeth. The back of the jaws had wide, flat, tilelike teeth. To capture prey such as a clam or mussel, *Placodus* would use its protruding front teeth to dig the bivalve mollusk out of the seafloor or to yank it from a rock to which it might have attached itself. The placodont then would position the bivalve between the large, flat teeth in the roof and floor of its mouth and use its powerful jaws to crush prey. Once the prey was crushed, the placodont would spit out the shell and swallow the soft parts of the animal that had been hidden inside.

Among the armored-plated placodonts were several members that resembled, but were not directly related to, turtles. *Cyamodus*, from the Middle Triassic of Germany, had a wide but short skull with a greatly reduced snout and face. Its front teeth were small, and it had a wide, flattened body with extensive armor that consisted of a carapace made up of hexagonal and rounded plates.

Nothosauria (Early to Late Triassic): Nothosaurs were better adapted to aquatic life than were placodonts. They had elongated bodies with long necks and tails and had powerful paddles for swimming. Although nothosaurs became extinct by the end of the Triassic, they appear to have been the ancestral stock from which the more streamlined and successful plesiosaurs arose, late in the Triassic. Nothosaur remains are limited almost exclusively to ancient ocean deposits in Europe, although a few remains have been found in China and Israel.

Most nothosaurs were only about three feet (1 m) long, although several larger kinds existed that measured about 10 to 13 feet (3 to 4 m). The neck and tail of a nothosaur were often about the same length, as in *Nothosaurus* and *Ceresiosaurus* ("Lake Lugano lizard"). Tails became shorter in many of the later plesiosaurs, giving them better speed and maneuverability in the water.

Nothosaurs were fish eaters; this becomes all the more evident when their jaws and teeth are examined. The front of the nothosaur snout was somewhat broad and spoon shaped. The upper and lower jaws were filled with long, curved, needlelike teeth that were widely spaced. The teeth interlocked when the jaws were closed; this made them excellent tools for clamping down on fish. The feet of the early nothosaurs, such as *Nothosaurus* and *Lariosaurus*, were webbed but still very reptilelike. (The name *Lariosaurus* comes from the Latin name for Lake Como, in Italy, *Lacus Larius*.) Later nothosaurs, including *Ceresiosaurus*, developed longer toes and more paddlelike feet. The forelimbs of nothosaurs were often larger and stronger than their hind limbs. This suggests that the forelimbs had a role in swimming, providing forward thrust and helping the animal to negotiate turns effectively.

Ichthyosauria (Early Triassic to Middle Cretaceous): Ichthyosaurs—the "fish lizards"—were one of the first fossil creatures to attract scientific attention. An illustration of one was published as early as 1699, but the bones were believed to be those of a fish. Everything understood at the time about fishes and reptiles would certainly make these swimming creatures appear, to most observers, to be fish. The fish theory prevailed for more than a hundred years, even after several more fossil remains were discovered. It was not until 1814 that the reknowned French anatomist Georges Cuvier (1769–1832) revealed the reptilian nature of ichthyosaurs by comparing the features of their skull and skeletal elements to those of other vertebrates. This was a startling conclusion at the time, 28 years before the word "dinosaur" was invented to describe the remains of several land-going extinct creatures.

Ichthyosaurs were dolphinlike in appearance but unrelated to those marine mammals. Ichthyosaurs have been found in many parts of the world, and they thrived throughout most of the age of dinosaurs. Some measured as small as six feet (1.8 m) long, but the group also included the largest ancient marine reptile of all—an ichthyosaur that measured an astounding 77 feet (23 m) long. That is longer than a sperm whale.

All ichthyosaurs had four side fins. Two, called forefins, were in front, next to the chest; the other two, called hindfins, were in the rear, next to the hip. The forefins were always larger than the hindfins. Later ichthyosaurs from the Jurassic also had a dorsal fin on the back, similar to that seen on a shark. Ichthyosaurs propelled themselves either by undulating the body or by waving the tail from side to side. Fins provided the animal with control over steering and balance, allowing it to stay upright, go up and down, and make turns.

Ichthyosaurs achieved their greatest diversity and numbers during the Jurassic Period.

Plesiosauria (Late Triassic to Late Cretaceous): Joining the ichthyosaurs in dominating the Mesozoic oceans were the plesiosaurs, a widespread and successful group of long- and short-necked predators that fed on fish, squid, and other swimmers.

Plesiosaurs are classified in two groups, based on the relative lengths of their necks. The long-necked plesiosaurs, although streamlined, may not have been skilled at high-speed chases of prey because movement of their heads may have caused the animals to change course. Instead, long-necked plesiosaurs may have hunted using an ambush style, waiting for fish to pass and then lashing out to snare them with their wicked teeth. The ambush technique also would have permitted the plesiosaur to conceal its body behind a rock or other obstacle, out of the view of approaching fishes. While intriguing, the ambush technique seems unlikely to some scientists because of the huge body size of these animals.

The short-necked plesiosaurs fell into several families, including the massive pliosaurs. Short-necked plesiosaurs were fearsome creatures—the top predators in their underwater world. With their large heads and streamlined bodies, pliosaurs were capable of quick movement and of sustained chases at high speed. Unlike the long-necked plesiosaur ambush hunters, pliosaurs probably were pursuit predators, chasing down large prey until they could snatch them in their jaws. Pliosaurs had sturdy, pointed teeth that were cone-shaped and abrasive, capable of cutting through thick flesh and even bones. The animals' mouths were huge. This made any sea creature of the time a potential meal, including the long-necked plesiosaurs, ichthyosaurs, giant squid, sharks, and the largest fish of the time. Pliosaurs probably filled an ecological niche similar to that of killer whales today. Among the largest pliosaurs were *Kronosaurus* (Australia), which was 42 feet (13 m) long, and *Liopleurodon* (England, Germany, France, and Russia), which was about 40 feet (12 m) long.

One reason that reptiles were able to become fully terrestrial was that they had developed the amniotic egg, which could be laid and fertilized outside of the water. While many marine reptiles probably continued this strategy of leaving the water to lay their eggs, the fishlike ichthyosaurs were clearly not capable of crawling onto land to complete this critical chore. Ichthyosaurs solved this problem by evolving the ability to retain their "eggs" inside the body and then give birth to live young when the eggs hatched. Several remarkable fossil specimens of ichthyosaurs either show unborn babies in the mothers' body cavities or show a baby ichthyosaur emerging tail first from the birth canal, its head still inside the mother.

INTO THE MESOZOIC ERA

The evolution of the amniotic egg gave vertebrates an adaptive advantage. It allowed them to exploit habitats beyond those of their waterbound amphibian ancestors. As a result, the first reptiles rapidly diversified into a variety of distinct families, each with its own peculiarities.

Vertebrate innovations seemed limitless as the Earth entered the Mesozoic Era. Even though the first reptiles were predators, many forms took advantage of the increasingly abundant plants in their world and developed highly specialized jaws, teeth, and chewing mechanisms to capitalize on this new food source. The reptilian backbone became stronger and more flexible, capable of supporting larger and faster species. The skull became lighter but also added important new nooks and crannies for the attachment of increasingly effective jaw muscles. The roof of the mouth developed a separate chamber, connected to the nostrils, to allow an animal to eat and breathe more efficiently at the same time. Legs became stronger and more flexible and were positioned further underneath the body, where they provided a more upright posture and the ability to run without dragging the belly. Some vertebrates developed longer hind limbs than forelimbs, the first step toward bipedalism in later vertebrates, including dinosaurs and mammals.

So numerous were the anatomical adaptations of the early reptiles that they diverged into widely different body plans and habitats on land and in the sea. By the Middle Triassic, the evolutionary stage was set for the rise of many new and distinct species. From the anapsids would arise one of the longest-standing branches of reptiles, the turtles and tortoises. The diapsids would offer up not only the dinosaurs, but also the first flying reptiles, the lizards, the snakes, and the birds. The euryapsid marine reptiles succeeded throughout the Mesozoic, staking their claim as the top predators of the seas. The synapsids, however, took an even more radical route away from their reptilian roots. After the demise of the sailbacked meat eaters and hulking hippopotamus-sized plant eaters of the Late Paleozoic, one branch of synapsids, the cynodonts, found a new formula for success in small size. While living in the shadows of larger and more formidable creatures, the cynodonts developed specializations that led to the appearance of the first mammals. The groundwork was laid for an extraordinary diversification of vertebrates throughout the rest of the Mesozoic Era.

SUMMARY

This chapter reviews the rise of the four main groups of amniotic vertebrates that closed the Paleozoic Era and led to the rise of reptiles as the dominant life-form of the Mesozoic Era.

1. A key diagnostic trait used to classify amniotes is a feature of the skull called the temporal fenestrae; these were openings, or "windows," in the skull, just behind the orbits, on the sides of the skull, or temple region.

2. Amniotes can be placed into one of four groups based on skull design: anapsids (no temporal fenestrae); synapsids (one temporal fenestra on each side); diapsids (two temporal fenestrae on each side); euryapsids (one highly placed temporal fenestra).

3. The earliest reptiles, including *Hylonomus* and *Paleothyris*, were anapsids. They were small insectivores that lived among the vegetative debris and tree stumps of the Middle Carboniferous forest. The anapsids also included the pareiasaurs, some of the earliest reptiles that were highly adapted for eating plants.

4. Early, successful synapsids included the sailback predator *Dimetrodon* and the plant-eating sailbacked *Edaphosaurus*. Later synapsids included the cynodonts, the ancestors of mammals.

5. Changes to the configuration of bones in the lower jaw of synapsids led to improved hearing and to a new form of flexible jaw joint that improved the way food could be chewed.

6. The diapsids are the most successful radiation of reptile forms. The diapsids are divided into two large groups: The archosaurs include crocodiles, birds, and extinct dinosaurs and pterosaurs. The lepidosaurs include lizards, snakes, two species of *Sphenodon*—the "living fossil" tuatara—and extinct mosasaurs.

7. The euryapsids included four groups of extinct marine reptiles, the placodonts, the nothosaurs, the ichthyosaurs, and the plesiosaurs.

CONCLUSION

Extinctions and the Amniotes: Shifting Opportunities for Tetrapods

March Onto Land has traced the transformation of Earth's terrestrial environments into a greening world that invited many kinds of organisms to leave their aquatic haven for new, unexplored territory. Plants in the form of algae made the first critical step; they were followed by arthropods as the land became increasingly green with new kinds of vegetation. The spread of the arthropods—including scorpions, spiders, and insects—was soon followed by the early tetrapods, the first vertebrates to step out of the water.

Tetrapods had opportunities on land, where they found themselves at the top of an untapped food chain of small arthropods and plants. Amphibians were the first vertebrate conquerors of the land, despite their need to return to the water to reproduce. This lifestyle was workable during the warm and wet Carboniferous Period. From the amphibians arose another line of tetrapods, a group of animals that were even better adapted for life on the land. These creatures, the amniotes, developed a way to lay their eggs out of the water. This freed them from oceans, lakes, and streams and allowed them to more fully explore and adapt to Earth's vast terrestrial resources.

Of the many remarkable evolutionary stories of the Paleozoic Era, probably none is more important to humans than the appearance of the synapsids—mammal-like reptiles. In their ancestry are found the first traces of mammals and the beginning of a long line of evolutionary changes that would produce a dazzling array of mammals, including the first primates and humans some 300 million years later.

The foundation for all terrestrial organisms, plants and animals alike, was laid down in the Paleozoic Era. The forward momentum of life, however, is sometimes inexplicably interrupted by natural events over which that life has no control. Such was the case 251 million years ago, when nearly all life became extinct. The worldwide extinctions at the end of the Permian Period hit the land and the sea with equal force. This geologic catastrophe was triggered by massive and prolonged volcanic activity in Siberia, a runaway **greenhouse effect**, and the plummeting of worldwide oxygen levels due to the disruption of Earth's natural **global chemostat**. The extinctions played out over a span of 500,000 years, severely challenging organisms of all kinds and fundamentally changing the history of life on Earth.

Fossil evidence shows that as much as 95 percent of all ocean species were erased during the end-Permian extinction. Gone from the oceans were most crinoids, brachiopods, reef-building bryozoans, nautiloids, and ammonoids: Nearly all marine invertebrate groups suffered huge losses and never regained the diversity that they once had. There, 75 percent of all terrestrial vertebrate taxa were wiped out. Among the animals eradicated were six families of archaic vertebrates that represented early amphibians, reptiles, and synapsids, including several families of formidable saurian predators. Whatever specializations evolution had fine-tuned in these creatures suddenly meant nothing. A small community of surviving species was left to shape the future of life.

By the Early Triassic Epoch, tetrapod communities had been devastated by extinction and were much less diverse. Gone were the sailbacked synapsids. Gone were the rhinoceros-sized, plant-eating pareiasaurs. All but a few lines of amphibians survived, however, as did a handful of hearty synapsid species. These synapsid survivors, including *Lystrosaurus* and the cynodont ancestors of mammals, continued to spread to far corners of the globe. The once-diverse

Permian oasis or hunting ground? A group of herbivorous Estemmenosuchus drink from a watering hole while the predatory Eotitanosuchus assesses his chances for making a kill.

anapsids, including ancestral turtles, merely stumbled into the Mesozoic Era after losing most of their numbers.

The earliest diapsids—then a line of small, swift, long-legged insect eaters—had lived in the shadows of more dominant creatures for much of the Permian Period. They, too, survived the end-Permian extinction. Changes to Earth's habitats following the Permian extinction included a shift from a warm and humid climate to one that was hotter and drier, as well as a shift in vegetation away from low-growing seed ferns to gymnosperms and taller conifers. By the end of the Triassic Period, it was clear that the diapsids were more able than other amniotes to adapt to these changes in climate and food supply, and a dramatic shift in faunal composition took place. Diapsids—dinosaurs and their kin—gradually replaced the once-dominant synapsids.

Because of the end-Permian mass extinction, the changeover from the Paleozoic Era to the Mesozoic Era also marked the end of many kinds of archaic life-forms and the beginning of new orders of life that are still represented by organisms living today. This is true for plants and invertebrates, but it is also significant to the evolution of vertebrates. By the end of the Mesozoic Era, all modern forms of vertebrates had firmly taken root. The Mesozoic Era is known today as the age of reptiles because life on land, in the sea, and in the air was ruled by the archosaurs. These included dinosaurs, marine reptiles, and flying reptiles. Sharing the world of the archosaurs and continuing to prosper and diversify in the shadows of giants were fishes, mammals, amphibians, and birds.

APPENDIX ONE:
GEOLOGIC TIME SCALE

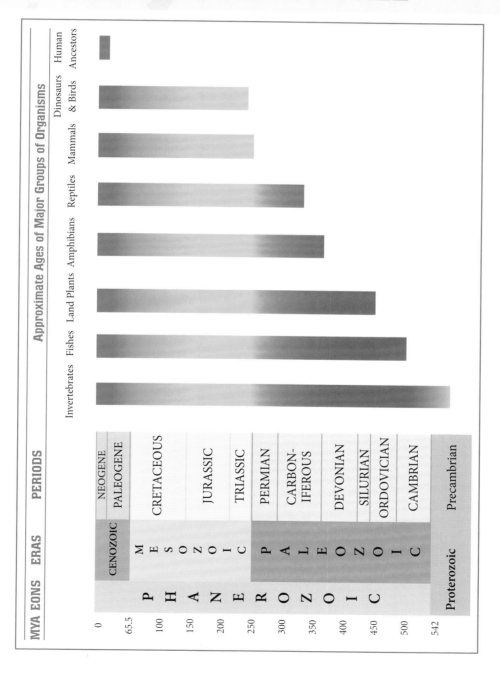

Approximate Ages of Major Groups of Organisms

MYA	EONS	ERAS	PERIODS
0		CENOZOIC	NEOGENE
			PALEOGENE
65.5			CRETACEOUS
100	PHANEROZOIC	MESOZOIC	
150			JURASSIC
200			
250			TRIASSIC
		PALEOZOIC	PERMIAN
300			CARBON-IFEROUS
350			
400			DEVONIAN
450			SILURIAN
			ORDOVICIAN
500			CAMBRIAN
542	Proterozoic		Precambrian

Column labels for organism bars: Invertebrates, Fishes, Land Plants, Amphibians, Reptiles, Mammals, Dinosaurs & Birds, Human Ancestors

APPENDIX TWO:
ANATOMICAL DIRECTIONS

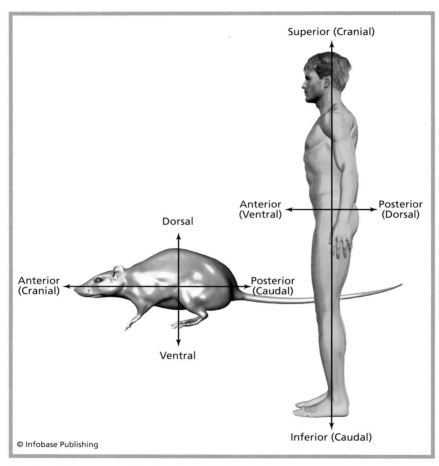

Superior (Cranial)

Anterior
(Ventral)

Posterior
(Dorsal)

Dorsal

Anterior
(Cranial)

Posterior
(Caudal)

Ventral

Inferior (Caudal)

© Infobase Publishing

Positional terms used to describe vertebrate anatomy

GLOSSARY

adaptations Changes in a lineage of organisms in response to environmental stress.

Amniota Vertebrate group that includes the most recent common ancestors of living reptiles, mammals, birds, and all their descendants.

amniote A tetrapod that protects the embryo of its offspring within the sealed environment of an amniotic egg; reptiles, mammals, and birds are amniotes.

amphibians Partly aquatic tetrapods that must return to the water to reproduce; amphibians hatch from eggs in the water and live a fully aquatic lifestyle until they reach sexual maturity.

Anapsida (diapsids) Amniotes with no temporal fenestrae, including the earliest reptiles.

anatomy Term used to describe the basic biological systems of an animal, such as the skeletal and muscular systems.

angiosperms The flowering plants.

anterior Directional term indicating the head end of a vertebrate, also known as the cranial end.

Archosauria The branch of diapsid reptiles that includes dinosaurs, pterosaurs, crocodiles, birds, and their kin.

arthropods (Arthropoda) Animal phylum whose members have a segmented body, body regions dedicated to specific functions, a jointed exoskeleton, and a nervous system on the underside of the body; arthropods include trilobites, crabs, lobsters, brine shrimp, barnacles, insects, spiders, scorpions, and centipedes.

basal At the base or earliest level of evolutionary development; a term usually used to refer to an ancestral taxon.

biramous Word used to describe double-branched arthropod limbs.

buccal pumping Method of breathing used by amphibians, in which air is sucked into the throat and then squeezed down the throat into the lungs by raising the floor of the mouth.

clade A group of related organisms including all the descendants of a single common ancestor

climate   The kind of weather that occurs at a particular place over time.

conducting system   System of veins in a vascular plant used to transport water and food.

continental drift   The slow and gradual movement and transformation of the continents due to shifting of the tectonic plates of Earth's crust.

coprolite   Fossilized animal feces.

costal ventilation   Method of breathing in tetrapods in which abdominal muscles and the rib cage expand and contract the lungs, forcing air in and out.

craton   The large, tectonically stable interior of a continent.

cuticle   The waxy outer covering of a plant.

derived   Term used to describe a trait of an organism that is a departure from the most primitive, or basal, form.

dermal   Pertaining to the skin, as in dermal armor.

desiccation   Water loss in the body due largely to evaporation.

Diapsida   (diapsids) Amniotes with two temporal fenestrae: a lower one like the one seen in synapsids and an upper one just above the lower one and behind the orbit.

ecosystem   A population of all living organisms and the environment in which they live.

ectothermic   Word used to describe a cold-blooded creature that regulates its body temperature by absorbing heat from its environment.

endoskeleton   An internal skeleton, usually consisting of bones, as is found in vertebrates.

endothermy   The state of being warm-blooded.

era   A span of geologic time ranking below the eon; the Archean Eon is divided into four eras dating from more than 4 billion years ago to 2.5 billion years ago; the Proterozoic Eon is divided into three eras dating from 2.5 billion years ago to about 542 million years ago; the Phanerozoic Eon is divided into three eras, the Paleozoic, the Mesozoic, and the Cenozoic; the Paleozoic ("ancient life") Era lasted from 542 million to 251 million years ago; the Mesozoic ("middle life") Era lasted from 251 million to 65 million years ago; the Cenozoic ("recent life") Era began 65 million years ago and continues to the present.

Eukarya   One of the three domains of living organisms; it includes four kingdoms—Protista, Fungi, Plantae, and Animalia—all of which consist of multicelled organisms with a distinct cell structure whose nucleus contains strands of DNA.

eukaryotes   Multicelled organisms with a distinct cell structure whose nucleus contains strands of DNA.

Euryapsida   (euryaspids) Amniotes with one temporal fenestra positioned just above and behind the orbit.

evolution   The natural process that causes species to change gradually over time; evolution is controlled by changes to the genetic code—the DNA—of organisms.

exoskeleton   A skeleton that forms on the outside of the body, as in invertebrates such as anthropods.

extant   Term used to describe an organism that is living today.

extinction   The irreversible elimination of an entire species of plant or animal because the species cannot adapt effectively to changes in its environment.

fauna   Animals found in a given ecosystem.

forelimbs   The two front legs of a vertebrate.

fossil   Any physical trace of prehistoric life.

gene   A microscopic unit on a DNA molecule that controls inherited traits.

genera   A taxonomic name for one or more closely related organisms; in taxonomic classification, genera rank below families and above species; the singular of the plural *genera* is *genus*.

gigantism   Inherited traits for unusually large growth, made possible through natural selection, for a taxon or taxa of organisms.

global chemostat   A complex, self-regulatory system by which the ocean naturally maintains its optimum chemical balance.

greenhouse effect   The trapping of reflected solar radiation by water vapor in clouds, ozone in the lower atmosphere, and atmospheric methane and carbon dioxide (CO_2) gas.

gymnosperms   Seed plants, such as conifers, that have a protective cone or other body for their seed embryos.

herbivory   The eating of plants and the anatomical adaptations that make this possible.

hind limbs   The two rear legs of a vertebrate.

index fossils   Fossils that are widely distributed and easily recognized but that are restricted to certain geologic strata; these qualities make such fossils useful for dating related stratigraphic layers around the Earth.

Lepidosauria   A group of diapsid reptiles that includes lizards, snakes, two species of *Sphenodon*—the lizardlike tuatara of New Zealand—and their extinct kin.

lycopods   A taxon of early seedless vascular plants that grew to tree height.

mass extinction   An extinction event that kills off more than 25 percent of all species in a million years or less.

microbiotic crusts   Matlike, terrestrial communities of fungi, algae, and bacteria whose filamentous structures trap small particles of sand and silt to form a soil surface.

morphological   Pertaining to the body form and structure of an organism.

natural selection   One of Charles Darwin's observations regarding the way evolution works; given the complex and changing conditions under which life exists, those individuals with the most favorable combination of inherited traits may survive and reproduce while others may not.

nonvascular plant   A plant that lacks vascular or conducting tissue for transporting water and food.

notochord   A stiff rod running along the back of an organism, found in members of the phylum Chordata.

orbit   An opening for the eye in the skull.

organism   Any living plant, animal, bacterium, archaebacterium, protist, or fungus.

ozone   A natural filter in Earth's lower atmosphere that prevents most of the deadly ultraviolet radiation from the Sun from striking the surface ground; ozone is made by a reaction that takes place when ultraviolet radiation from the Sun strikes oxygen molecules, splitting them apart and recombining with other elements in the atmosphere to form a protective gaseous band around the planet.

paleontologist   A scientist who studies prehistoric life, often using fossils.

period   A span of geologic time ranking below the era; the Phanerozoic Eon is divided into three eras and 11 periods, each covering a span of millions of years; the longest of these periods, including the three in the Mesozoic Era, are sometimes further broken down into smaller divisions of time.

photosynthesis   A metabolic process in which an organism's cells convert energy from the Sun, carbon dioxide, and water to reproduce their cells; the waste product of photosynthesis is free oxygen released into the atmosphere.

physiology   The way in which an animal's parts work together and are adapted to help the organism survive.

population   Members of the same species that live in a particular area.

predator   An animal that actively seeks and feeds on other live animals.

progymnosperms   Seedless vascular plants that reproduced by spores like seedless ferns but that had a woody bark as a protective covering like typical conifers.

seedless vascular plants   Vascular plants that reproduce by means of spores instead of seeds.

species   In classification, the most basic biological unit of living organisms; members of a species can interbreed and produce fertile offspring.

stapes   A bone of the middle ear of vertebrates that aids in hearing.

stomata   A network of tiny pores on the outside surface of a plant for collecting oxygen from the air; the stomata are part of the gas-exchange system of a plant that makes photosynthesis possible.

Synapsida   (synapsids) Amniotes with one temporal fenestra positioned somewhat behind and below each orbit.

taxon   (plural: taxa) In classification, a group of related organisms such as a clade, genus, or species.

taxonomy   The science of classifying living and extinct species of organisms.

temporal fenestrae   Openings, or "windows," in the vertebrate skull, just behind the orbit on each side, or temple region, of the skull.

tetrapods   Vertebrate animals with four limbs, or their evolutionary descendants that have modified or lost limbs, including all amphibians, reptiles, mammals, and birds.

Tetrapoda   A group that includes the common ancestor of all living tetrapods and all of its descendants.

Therapsida   (therapsids) A group of synapsid reptiles, including the ancestors of the first mammals.

thermoregulation   The control of body temperature.

trace fossil   A type of fossil that preserves evidence of the presence of a prehistoric organism but does not include body parts; fossilized trackways or feces are examples of trace fossils.

tracheal system   The respiratory system of a terrestrial organism, used to consume oxygen from the air.

trackway   The fossilized footprints or markings left by a prehistoric animal.

transitional   Word used to describe a fossil that represents intermediate conditions in the evolution of a species.

ultraviolet solar radiation   Ultraviolet light emitted by the Sun that can be harmful to organisms even if it is not screened by Earth's ozone layer.

uniramous   Word used to describe single-branched arthropod limbs.

vascular plant   A plant that has a conducting system of veins to transport water and food throughout its body.

Chapter Bibliography

Preface

Wilford, John Noble. "When No One Read, Who Started to Write?" *The New York Times*, April, 6, 1999. Available online. URL: http://query.nytimes.com/gst/fullpage.html?res=9B01EFD61139F935A35757C0A9 6F958260. Accessed October 8, 2007.

Chapter 1 – Paleozoic Terrestrial Environments

Algeo, Thomas J., and Stephen E. Scheckler. "Terrestrial-Marine Teleconnections in The Devonian: Links Between the Evolution of Land Plants, Weathering Processes, and Marine Anoxic Events." *Philosophical Transactions of the Royal Society of London* (1998): 113–130.

Berner, Robert A. "Atmospheric Oxygen Over Phanerozoic Time." *Proceedings of the National Academy of Sciences of the United States of America* 96, no. 20 (September 28, 1999): 10955–10957

Chumakov, N.M. . "Trends in Global Climate Changes Inferred from Geological Data." *Stratigraphy and Geological Correlation* 12, no. 2 (2004): 7–32.

Ellis, Richard. *No Turning Back: The Life and Death of Animal Species.* New York: Harper Collins, 2004.

Goddéris, Yves, Louis M. François, and Ján Veizer. "The Early Paleozoic Carbon Cycle." *Earth and Planetary Science Letters* no. 190 (2001): 181–196.

Jacobs, David K., and David R. Lindberg. "Oxygen and Evolutionary Patterns in the Sea: Onshore/Offshore Trends and Recent Recruitment of Deep-Sea Faunas." *Proceedings of the National Academy of Sciences of the United States of America* 95 (August 1998): 9396–9401.

Kious, W. Jacquelyne, and Robert I. Tilling. *This Dynamic Earth: The Story of Plate Tectonics.* Washington: The United States Geological Survey, 2001.

Palmer, Douglas. *Atlas of the Prehistoric World.* New York: Discovery Books, 1999.

Pechenik, Jan A. *Biology of the Invertebrates*, 5th ed. New York: McGraw-Hill, 2005.

Plummer, Charles C., David McGeary, and Diane H. Carlson. *Physical Geology*. New York: McGraw-Hill, 2005.

Prothero, Donald R., and Robert H. Dott Jr. *Evolution of the Earth*, 7th ed. New York: McGraw-Hill, 2004.

Raup, David M. *Extinction: Bad Genes or Bad Luck?* New York: W.W. Norton, 1991.

———. *The Nemesis Affair*. New York: W.W. Norton, 1986.

Saltzman, Barry. *Dynamical Paleoclimatology: Generalized Theory of Global Climate Change*, New York: Academic Press, 2002.

Shear, William A. "The Early Development of Terrestrial Ecosystems." *Nature* 351 (May 23, 1991): 283–289.

Sidor, Christian A., F. Robin O'Keefe, Ross Damiani, J. Sébastien Steyer, Roger M.H. Smith, Hans C.E. Larsson, Paul C. Sereno, Oumarou Ide, and Abdoulaye Maga. "Permian Tetrapods from the Sahara Show Climate-Controlled Endemism in Pangaea." *Nature* 434 (April 14, 2005): 886–889.

Chapter 2 – The First Land Plants

Beerling, D.J., C.P. Osborne, and W.G. Chaloner. "Evolution of Leaf-Form in Land Plants Linked to Atmospheric CO_2 Decline in the Late Paleozoic Era." *Nature* 410 (March 15, 2001): 352–354.

Crane, Peter R., Else Marie Frils, and Kaj Raunsgaard Pedersen. "The Origin and Early Diversification of Angiosperms." *Nature* 374 (March 2, 1995): 27–33.

DiMichele, William A., Hermann W. Pfefferkorn, and Robert A. Gastaldo. "Response of Late Carboniferous and Early Permian Plant Communities to Climate Change." *Annual Review of Earth and Planetary Sciences* 29 (May 2001): 461–487.

Fleming, P.J.G., and J.F. Rigby. "Possible Land Plants from the Middle Cambrian, Queensland." *Nature* 238 (August 4, 1972): 266.

Kenrick, Paul. "Turning Over a New Leaf." *Nature* 410 (March 15, 2001): 309–310.

Kenrick, Paul, and Peter R. Crane. "The Origin and Early Evolution of Plants on Land." *Nature* 389 (September 4, 1997): 33–39.

Koch, George W., Stephen C. Sillett, Gregory M. Jennings, and Stephen D. Davis. "The Limits to Tree Height." *Nature* 428 (April 22, 2004): 851–854.

Mapes, Gene, Far W. Rothwell, and M.T. Haworth. "Evolution of Seed Dormancy." *Nature* 337 (February 16, 1989): 645–646.

Niklas, Karl J., Bruce H. Tiffney, and Andrew H. Knoll. "Patterns in Vascular Land Plant Diversification." *Nature* 303 (June 16, 1983): 614–616.

Osborne, C.P., D.J. Beerling, B.H. Lomax, and W.G. Chaloner. "Biophysical Constraints on the Origin of Leaves Inferred from the Fossil Record." *Proceedings of the National Academy of Sciences of the United States of America* 101, no. 28 (July 13, 2004): 10360–10362.

Prothero, Donald R., and Robert H. Dott Jr. *Evolution of the Earth*, 7th ed. New York: McGraw-Hill, 2004.

Qiu, Yin-Long, Jungho Lee, Fabiana Bernasconi-Quadroni, Douglas E. Soltis, Pamela S. Soltis, Michael Zanis, Elizabeth A. Zimmer, Zhiduan Chen, Vincent Savolainen, and Mark W. Chase. "The Earliest Angiosperms: Evidence from Mitochondrial, Plastid and Nuclear Genomes." *Nature* 402 (November 25, 1999): 404–407.

Schneider, Harald, Eric Schuettpelz, Kathleen M. Pryer, Raymond Cranfill, Susana Magallón, and Richard Lupia. "Ferns Diversified in the Shadow of Angiosperms." *Nature* 428 (April 1, 2004): 553–557.

Shear, William A. "The Early Development of Terrestrial Ecosystems." *Nature* 351 (May 23, 1991): 283–289.

Stern, Kingley R. *Introductory Plant Biology*, 10th ed. New York: McGraw-Hill, 2006.

Uno, Gordon, Richard Storey, and Randy Moore. *Principles of Botany*. New York: McGraw-Hill, 2001.

Wilf, Peter. "When Are Leaves Good Thermometers? A New Case for Leaf Margin Analysis." *Paleobiology* 23, no. 3 (1997): 373–390.

Wolfe, J.A. "Paleoclimatic Estimates from Tertiary Leaf Assemblages. *Annual Reviews of Earth and Planetary Science* 23 (1995): 119–142.

Zhou, Zhiyan, and Shaolin Zheng. "The Missing Link in Ginkgo Evolution." *Nature* 423 (June 19, 2003): 821–822.

Chapter 3 – The First Land Animals

Averof, Michael, and Stephen M. Cohen. "Evolutionary Origin of Insect Wings from Ancestral Gills." *Nature* 385 (February 13, 1997): 627–630.

Budd, Graham E., Anette E.S. Högström, and Ivan Gogin. "A Myriapod-Like Arthropod from the Upper Cambrian of East Siberia." *Palaeontologische Zeitschrift* 75, no. 1 (2001): 37–41.

Dudley, Robert. "Atmospheric Oxygen, Giant Paleozoic Insects and the Evolution of Aerial Locomotor Performance." *Journal of Experimental Biology* 201 (1998): 1043–1050.

Dunlop, Jason A. "A Trigonotarbid Arachnid from the Upper Silurian of Shropshire." *Palaeontology* 39 (1996): 605–614.

Dunlop, Jason A., and Ronny Röbler. "The Trigonotarbid Arachnid *Anthracomartus voelkelianus* (Anthracomartidae)." *Journal of Arachnology* 30, no. 2 (2002): 211–218.

Edgecombe, Gregory D. "Devonian Terrestrial Arthropods from Gondwana." *Nature* 394 (July 9, 1998): 172–175.

Engel, Michael S., and David A. Grimaldi. "New Light Shed on the Oldest Insect." *Nature* 427 (February 12, 2004): 627–630.

Fortey, Richard. *Life: A Natural History of the First Four Billion Years of Life on Earth.* New York: Alfred A. Knopf, 1998.

Gorder, Pam Frost. "Largest Fossil Cockroach Found; Site Preserves Incredible Detail." Ohio State Research Communications (November 7, 2001). Available online. URL: http://researchnews.osu.edu/archive/bigroach.htm. Accessed November 6, 2007.

Grimaldi, David. "Insect Evolutionary History from Handlirsch to Hennig and Beyond." *Journal of Paleontology* 75, no. 6 (2001): 1152–1160.

Grimaldi, David, and Michael S. Engel. *Evolution of the Insects.* Cambridge: Cambridge University Press, 2005.

Humphreys, Geoff S. "Evolution of Terrestrial Burrowing Invertebrates." *Advances in Regolith* (2003): 211–215.

Jeram, Andrew J. "Book Lungs in a Lower Carboniferous Scorpion." *Nature* 343 (January 25, 1990): 360–361.

Kowalewski, Michal, and Patricia H. Kelley, editors. *The Fossil Record of Predation: Methods, Patterns, and Processes.* Paleontological Society Special Papers 8 (2002): 395–398.

Miller, Stephen A., and John P. Harley. *Zoology*, 6th ed. New York: McGraw-Hill, 2005.

Pechenik, Jan A. *Biology of the Invertebrates*, 5th ed. New York: McGraw-Hill, 2005.

Prothero, Donald R., and Robert H. Dott Jr. *Evolution of the Earth*, 7th ed. New York: McGraw-Hill, 2004.

Raven, Peter H., George B. Johnson, Jonathan B. Losos, and Susan R. Singer. *Biology,* 7th ed. New York: McGraw-Hill, 2005.

Rolfe, W.D. Ian. "Seeking the Arthropods of Eden." *Nature* 348 (November 8, 1990): 112–113.

Selden, Paul A., José A. Corronca, and Mario A. Hünicken. "The True Identity of the Supposed Giant Fossil Spider *Megarachne*." Biology Letters 1, no. 1 (March 22, 2005): 44–48.

Shear, William A., and J. Kukalova-Peck. "The Ecology of Paleozoic Terrestrial Arthropods: The Fossil Evidence." *Journal of Canadian Zoology* 68, no. 9 (1990): 1807–1834.

Shear, William A., Wolfgang Schawaller, and Patricia M. Bonamo. "Record of Palaeozoic Pseudoscorpions." *Nature* 341 (October 12, 1989): 527–529.

Shultz, Jeffrey W. "The Limits of Stratigraphic Evidence in Assessing Phylogenetic Hypotheses of Recent Arachnids." *Journal of Arachnology* 22 (1994): 169–172.

Whalley, Paul, and E.A. Jarzembowski. "A New Assessment of *Rhyniella*, the Earliest Known Insect, from the Devonian of Rhynie, Scotland." *Nature* 291 (May 28, 1981): 317.

Wootton, Robin J., and Jarmila Kukalova-Peck. "Flight Adaptations in Palaeozoic Palaeoptera (Insecta)" *Biology Review* 75 (2000): 129–167.

Chapter 4 – Going Ashore: Becoming a Land Animal

Ahlberg, Per E., and Jennifer A. Clack. "A Firm Step from Water to Land." *Nature* 440 (April 6, 2006): 747–749.

Ahlberg, Per E., and Zerina Johanson. "Osteolepiforms and the Ancestry of Tetrapods." *Nature* 395 (October 22, 1998): 792–794.

Ahlberg, Per E., and Andrew R. Milner. "The Origin and Early Diversification of Tetrapods." *Nature* 368 (April 7, 1994): 507–514.

Brazeau, Martin D., and Per E. Ahlberg. "Tetrapod-like Middle Ear Architecture in a Devonian Fish." *Nature* 439 (January 19, 2006): 318–321.

Clack, Jennifer A. "An Early Tetrapod from 'Romer's Gap.'" *Nature* 418 (July 2, 2002): 72–76.

———. "From Fins to Fingers." *Science* 304 (April 2, 2004): 57–58.

———. "Getting a Leg Up on Land." *Scientific American*, December 2005: 100–107.

———. "A New Early Carboniferous Tetrapod with a Mélange of Crown Group Characters." *Nature* 394 (July 2, 1998): 66–69.

———. *Gaining Ground: The Origin and Evolution of Tetrapods.* Bloomington: Indiana University Press, 2002.

Clack, Jennifer A., P.E. Ahlberg, S.M. Finney, P. Dominguez Alonso, J. Robinson, and R.A. Ketcham. "A Uniquely Specialized Ear in a Very Early Tetrapod." *Nature* 425 (September 4, 2003): 66–69.

Clément, Gaël, Per E. Ahlberg, Alain Blieck, Henning Blom, Jennifer A. Clack, Edouard Poty, Jacques Thorez, and Philippe Janvier. "Devonian Tetrapod from Western Europe." *Nature* 427 (January 29, 2004): 412–413.

Coates, M.I., and J.A. Clack. "Fish-like Gills and Breathing in the Earliest Known Tetrapod." *Nature* 352 (July 18, 1991): 234–236.

Graham, Jeffrey B., and Heather J. Lee. "Breathing Air in Air: In What Ways Might Extant Amphibious Fish Biology Relate to Prevailing Concepts About Early Tetrapods, the Evolution of Vertebrate Air Breathing, and the Vertebrate Land Transition?" *Physiological and Biochemical Zoology* 77 (2004): 720–731.

Graham, Jeffrey B., Robert Dudley, Nancy M. Aguilar, and Carl Gans. "Implications of the Late Paleozoic Oxygen Pulse for Physiology and Evolution." *Nature* 375 (May 11, 1995): 117–120.

Lebedev, Oleg A. "Fins Made for Walking." *Nature* 390 (November 6, 1997): 21–22.

Long, John A., and Malcolm S. Gordon. "The Greatest Step in Vertebrate History: A Paleobiological Review of the Fish-Tetrapod Transition." *Physiological and Biochemical Zoology* 77 (2004): 700–719.

Nelson, Laura. "Strong-arm Tactics Drove Creatures from the Pond." news@nature.com. Available online. URL: http://www.nature.com/news/2004/040329/full/news040329–16.html. Accessed November 6, 2007.

Norman, David. *Prehistoric Life: The Rise of the Vertebrates*. New York: Macmillan, 1994.

Raven, Peter H., George B. Johnson, Jonathan B. Losos, and Susan R. Singer. *Biology,* 7th ed. New York: McGraw-Hill, 2005.

Romer, Alfred Sherwood. *Man and the Vertebrates*. Chicago: University of Chicago Press, 1933.

———. *The Procession of Life; A World Natural History*. Cleveland: The World Publishing, 1968.

———. *The Vertebrate Story*, 4th ed. Chicago: University of Chicago Press, 1959.

Romer, Alfred Sherwood, and Thomas S. Parsons. *The Vertebrate Body, Shorter Version*, 5th ed. Philadelphia: W.B. Saunders, 1978.

Shimeld, Sebastian M., and Peter W.H. Holland. "Vertebrate Innovations." *Proceedings of the National Academy of Sciences of the United States of America* 97, no. 9 (April 25, 2000): 4449–4452.

Shubin, Neil H. "Evolutionary Cut and Paste." *Nature* 394 (July 2, 1998): 12–13.

Shubin, Neil. H., Edward B. Daeschler, and Farish A. Jenkins Jr. "The Pectoral Fin of *Tiktaalik rosae* and the Origin of the Tetrapod Limb." *Nature* 440 (April 6, 2006): 764–771.

Chapter 5 – The Diversity of Early Tetrapods

Bolt, John R., R.M. McKay, B.J. Witzke, and M.P. McAdams. "A New Lower Carboniferous Tetrapod Locality in Iowa." *Nature* 333 (June 23, 1988): 768–770.

Daeschler, Edward B. "Early Tetrapod Jaws from the Late Devonian of Pennsylvania, USA." *Journal of Paleontology* 74, no. 2 (2000): 301–308.

Daeschler, Edward B., and Neil Shubin. "Fish with Fingers?" *Nature* 391 (January 8, 1997): 133.

Daeschler, Edward B., Neil H. Shubin, and Farish A. Jenkins Jr. "A Devonian Tetrapod-like Fish and the Evolution of the Tetrapod Body Plan." *Nature* 440 (April 6, 2006): 757–763.

Fortey, Richard. *Life: A Natural History of the First Four Billion Years of Life on Earth*. New York: Alfred A. Knopf, 1998.

Milner, Andrew. "Late Extinctions of Amphibians." *Nature* 338 (March 9, 1989): 117.

Milner, Andrew R. "Scottish Window on Terrestrial Life in the Lower Carboniferous." *Nature* 314 (March 28, 1985): 320–321.

Norman, David. *Prehistoric Life: The Rise of the Vertebrates*. New York: Macmillan, 1994.

Sidor, Christian A., F. Robin O'Keefe, Ross Damiani, J. Sébastien Steyer, Roger M.H. Smith, Hans C.E. Larsson, Paul C. Sereno, Oumarou Ide, and Abdoulaye Maga. "Permian Tetrapods from the Sahara Show Climate-Controlled Endemism in Pangaea." *Nature* 434 (April 14, 2005): 886–889.

Thulborn, Tony, Anne Warren, Susan Turner, and Tim Hamley. "Early Carboniferous Tetrapods in Australia." *Nature* 381 (June 27, 1996): 777–780.

Wood, S.P., A.L. Panchen, and T.R. Smithson. "A Terrestrial Fauna from the Scottish Lower Carboniferous." *Nature* 314 (March 28, 1985): 355–356.

Zhu, Min, Per E. Ahlberg, Wenjin Zhao, and Liantao Jia. "First Devonian Tetrapod from Asia." *Nature* 420 (December 19/26, 2002): 760–761.

Chapter 6 – Taking Over the Land: Reptiles and Their Kin

Carroll, Robert. "Between Fish and Amphibian." *Nature* Vol. 373 (February 2, 1995): 389–390.

———. "Early Land Vertebrates." *Nature* 418 (July 4, 2002): 35–36.

Colbert, Edwin H., and Michael Morales. *Evolution of the Vertebrates,* 4th ed. New York: John Wiley & Sons, 1991.

Kemp, T.S. "Origin of Mammal-like Reptiles." *Nature* 283 (January 24, 1980): 378–380.

Norman, David. *Prehistoric Life: The Rise of the Vertebrates.* New York: Macmillan, 1994.

Romer, Alfred Sherwood, and Thomas S. Parsons. *The Vertebrate Body, Shorter Version*, 5th ed. Philadelphia: W.B. Saunders, 1978.

Storrs, Glenn. "Fossil Vertebrate Faunas of the British Rhaetian (latest Triassic)." *Zoological Journal of the Linnean Society* no. 112 (1994): 217–259.

Chapter 7 – Vertebrates Branch Out

Callaway, Jack M., and Elizabeth L. Nicholls, editors. *Ancient Marine Reptiles.* San Diego: Academic Press, 1997.

Darren Naish, "Placodonts: The Bizarre 'Walrus-Turtles' of the Triassic." Oceans of Kansas. Available online. URL: http://www.oceansofkansas.com/placodnt.html. Accessed November 6, 2007.

Edwards, Dianne, Paul A. Selden, John B. Richardson, and Lindsey Axe. "Coprolites as Evidence for Plant-Animal Interaction in Siluro-Devonian Terrestrial Ecosystems." *Nature* 377 (September 28, 1995): 329–331.

Everhart, Michael J. *Oceans of Kansas: A Natural History of the Western Interior Sea.* Bloomington: Indiana University Press, 2005.

Norman, David. *Prehistoric Life: The Rise of the Vertebrates.* New York: Macmillan, 1994.

Raven, Peter H., George B. Johnson, Jonathan B. Losos, and Susan R. Singer. *Biology,* 7th ed. New York: McGraw-Hill, 2005.

Romer, Alfred Sherwood, and Thomas S. Parsons. *The Vertebrate Body, Shorter Version*, 5th ed. Philadelphia: W.B. Saunders, 1978.

FURTHER READING

Benton, Michael. *Vertebrate Paleontology*, 3rd ed. Oxford: Blackwell Publishing, 2005.

Clack, Jennifer A. *Gaining Ground: The Origin and Evolution of Tetrapods*. Bloomington: Indiana University Press, 2002.

Ellis, Richard. *No Turning Back: The Life and Death of Animal Species*. New York: Harper Collins, 2004.

Fortey, Richard. *Life: A Natural History of the First Four Billion Years of Life on Earth*. New York: Alfred A. Knopf, 1998.

Gould, Stephen J., editor. *The Book of Life*. New York: W.W. Norton, 1993.

Grimaldi, David, and Michael S. Engel. *Evolution of the Insects*. Cambridge: Cambridge University Press, 2005.

Lambert, David. *Encyclopedia of Prehistory*. New York: Facts on File, 2002.

Margulis, Lynn, and Karlene V. Schwartz. *Five Kingdoms: An Illustrated Guide to the Phyla of Life on Earth*, 3rd ed. New York: W.H. Freeman, 1998.

Norman, David. *Prehistoric Life: The Rise of the Vertebrates*. New York: Macmillan, 1994.

Palmer, Douglas. *Atlas of the Prehistoric World*. New York: Discovery Books, 1999.

Pechenik, Jan A. *Biology of the Invertebrates*, 5th ed. New York: McGraw-Hill, 2005.

Plummer, Charles C., David McGeary, and Diane H. Carlson. *Physical Geology*. New York: McGraw-Hill, 2005.

Prothero, Donald R., and Robert H. Dott Jr. *Evolution of the Earth*. New York: McGraw-Hill, 2004.

Raven, Peter H., George B. Johnson, Jonathan B. Losos, and Susan R. Singer. *Biology*, 7th ed. New York: McGraw-Hill, 2005.

Saltzman, Barry. *Dynamical Paleoclimatology: Generalized Theory of Global Climate Change*. New York: Academic Press, 2002.

Stern, Kingley R. *Introductory Plant Biology*, 10th ed. New York: McGraw-Hill, 2006.

Web Sites

Academy of Natural Sciences of Philadelphia. Devonian Times

An online resource devoted to the evolution of tetrapods; provided by the Academy of Natural Sciences of Philadelphia, the home of Ted Daeshler, codiscoverer of *Tiktaalik*

http://www.devoniantimes.org/index.html

American Geological Institute. CUES: Constructing Understandings of Earth Systems

An interactive reference, provided by the American Geological Institute, to the primary systems that work together to make the world we know, including the geosphere, the hydrosphere, the atmosphere, and the biosphere

http://www.agiweb.org/education/cues/index.html

American Museum of Natural History. Life Forms

A guide to deep-sea hydrothermal animals, some of the most unusual and primitive creatures on the planet

http://www.amnh.org/nationalcenter/expeditions/blacksmokers/life_forms.html

Australian Museum. Palaeontology

Exhibits on the site include Australia's Lost Kingdoms, a photographic journey that explores early fossils and life-forms found in Australia.

http://www.austmus.gov.au/palaeontology/index.htm

Bernard Price Institute for Palaeontological Research, University of the Witwatersrand, Johannesburg. Fossil Picture Gallery

The Bernard Price Institute for Palaeontological Research provides information for a wide variety of South African vertebrate fossils.

http://www.wits.ac.za/geosciences/bpi/fossilpictures.htm

Dunlop, Jason. Arachnid Origins and Evolution

A Web site devoted to arachnid evolution, created by Dr. Jason Dunlop, curator of Chelicerata, Institut für Systematische Zoologie, Museum für Naturkunde, Berlin, Germany

http://members.tripod.com/~DrJasonDunlop/index.html

International Commission on Stratigraphy. International Stratigraphic Chart

Downloadable geologic time scales provided by the International Commission on Stratigraphy

http://www.stratigraphy.org/cheu.pdf

Kerp, Hans. A History of Palaeozoic Forests

Guide to the evolution of early land plants; sponsored by the Westfälische Wilhelms University in Münster, Germany, a leading center of paleobotanical research

http://www.uni-muenster.de/GeoPalaeontologie/Palaeo/Palbot/ewald.html

Kazlev, Alan and Augustus White. Palaeos: The Trace of Life on Earth

A robust and continuously growing reference about all kinds of life-forms

http://www.palaeos.com/

Lapworth Museum, University of Birmingham. Palaeontological Collections: Vertebrate Collection

Online exhibit exploring early vertebrate life, particularly fishes, from the United Kingdom

http://www.lapworth.bham.ac.uk/collections/palaeontology/vertebrates.htm

Maddison, D.R., and K.-S. Schulz. The Tree of Life Web Project

A meticulously designed view of life-forms based on their phylogenetic (evolutionary) connections. The site is hosted by the University of Arizona College of Agriculture and Life Sciences and the University of Arizona Library.

http://tolweb.org/tree/phylogeny.html

Paleontology Portal. Vertebrates

A resource that explores early vertebrate life; produced by the University of California Museum of Paleontology, the Paleontological Society, the Society of Vertebrate Paleontology, and the United States Geological Survey

http://www.paleoportal.org/index.php?globalnav=fossil_gallery&sectionnav=taxon&taxon_id=16

Peripatus, Chris. Paleontology Page

A privately compiled but exhaustive resource on many paleontology subjects, including a valuable look at the Burgess Shale fossils

http://www.peripatus.gen.nz/Paleontology/Index.html

Public Broadcasting Service. Evolution Library: Evidence for Evolution

This resource outlines the extensive evidence in support of both the fact and theory of evolution; the site's approach is based on studies of the fossil record, molecular sequences, and comparative anatomy.

http://www.pbs.org/wgbh/evolution/library/04/

Scotese, Christopher R. Paleomap Project

A valuable source of continental maps showing the positioning of Earth's continents over the course of geologic time

http://www.scotese.com/

University of Aberdeen. How Do We Study the Rhynie Chert?

A tutorial about the Rhynie Chert, developed by the University of Aberdeen in Scotland

http://www.abdn.ac.uk/rhynie/how.htm

University of California Museum of Paleontology. Transitional Forms

A tutorial about transitional forms in the fossil record, with illustrated examples

http://evolution.berkeley.edu/evosite/lines/IAtransitional.shtml

Virtual Fossil Museum. Fossils Across Geological Time and Evolution

A privately funded, image-rich educational resource dedicated to fossils. Contributors include amateur and professional paleontologists.

http://www.fossilmuseum.net/index.htm

PICTURE CREDITS

Page

INDEX

Cones, 51–53
Conifers, 38, 39, 51–53,
    55–56
Continental drift,
    23–26, 30
Cooksonia, 45, 46, 47, 49
Coprolites, 132
Cordaites, 51, 53
Costal ventilation, 93
Crassigyrinidae, 117
Cratons, 23–24, 32
Crustaceans, 57, 58, 82
Cuticle, 39, 56
Cuvier, Georges, 156
Cyamodontoidea,
    153–154
Cyamodus, 153, 154
Cyanobacteria, 28, 35–36
Cycads, 38, 39
Cynodonts, 144–147
Cynognathus, 147

D

Daeschler, Ted, 17,
    98–99, 105–107, 110,
    114–116
Darwin, Charles, 18
Dendrerpeton, 119–120
Dermal scales, 92
Desiccation, 39, 56
Detritus, 58, 67
Devonian Period, 22, 28
Diapsida, 17, 137–138,
    147–152
Dicynodonts, 143–144
Digits, tetrapods and,
    91–92
Dimetrodon, 140, 146,
    159
Dinocephalids,
    142–143
Diplocaulus, 121
Dipnoi (lungfishes), 93,
    96, 102, 104

Diptera, 64
Dogs, 147
Dragonflies, 64, 67–68,
    72, 84
Drought, adaptations to,
    97–98

E

Ears, 94, 146
Ectotherms, 140
Edaphosaurus, 140–141,
    159
Eggs, 127, 157
Elginerpeton, 103, 113
Elkinsia, 53, 54
Elpistostege, 103
Endotherms, 142
Engel, Michael, 66
Ensifera, 69
Eryopoidea, 122
Erythrosuchus, 150
Estemmenosuchus, 163
Eukarya, 35, 55
Euparkeria, 150–151
Euryapsida, 17, 138,
    152–157, 160
Eurypterids, 75–77
Eusthenopteron, 90, 94,
    104–105
Evergreen trees, 38, 39,
    55–56
Exoskeletons, 62, 71
Extinctions, mass, 17,
    22, 162
Eyes, 94–95, 136–137

F

Feeding, 31
Fenestrae, 136–138, 152,
    159
Ferns, 38, 39, 46, 47, 53
Fins, 86, 95–99, 156.
    See also Lobe-finned
    fishes

Fish, 23, 86–91, 95–100.
    See also Dipnoi; Lobe-
    finned fishes
Flight, 62, 73. *See also*
    Wings
Fortey, Richard, 62, 80
Fossils, 58, 71, 98
Frills, 150
Fruits, 38, 40
Fungi, 43

G

Gait, 146–147
Gametophytes, 51
Gases. *See also specific
    gases*
    arthropod gigantism
        and, 60–62
    evolution of leaves
        and, 49–50, 56
    insects and, 73–74
    life on land and,
        41, 42
    Paleozoic Era and,
        28–29, 32
Genes, 66
Genoa River trackways,
    103–104
Gigantism, 24, 29,
    60–62, 77, 84
Gilboa fauna, 59, 66
Gills, 60, 73, 75, 84
Glaciations, 24
Global chemostat, 162
Glossopteris, 51, 53–55
Gondwana, 23–24
Gravity, 88–92
Green algae, 35, 36,
    43, 55
Greenhouse effect,
    162
Greererpeton, 119
Grimaldi, David, 66
Ground cover, 26–27, 32

ABOUT THE AUTHOR

THOM HOLMES is a writer specializing in natural history subjects and dinosaurs. He is noted for his expertise on the early history of dinosaur science in America. He was the publications director of *The Dinosaur Society* for five years (1991–1997) and the editor of its newsletter, *Dino Times*, the world's only monthly publication devoted to news about dinosaur discoveries. It was through the Society and his work with the Academy of Natural Sciences in Philadelphia that Thom developed widespread contacts and working relationships with paleontologists and paleo-artists throughout the world.

Thom's published works include *Fossil Feud: The Rivalry of America's First Dinosaur Hunters* (Silver Burdett Press, September 1997); *The Dinosaur Library* (Enslow, *2001–2002*); *Duel of the Dinosaur Hunters* (Pearson Education, *2002*); and *Fossil Feud: The First American Dinosaur Hunters* (Silver Burdett/Julian Messner, 1997). His many honors and awards include the National Science Teachers Association's *Outstanding Science Book of 1998*, VOYA's 1997 Non-fiction Honor List, an Orbis Pictus Honor, and the Chicago Public Library Association's *"Best of the Best"* in science books for young people.

Thom did undergraduate work in geology and studied paleontology through his role as a staff educator with the Academy of Natural Sciences in Philadelphia. He is a regular participant in field exploration, with two recent expeditions to Patagonia in association with Canadian, American, and Argentinian universities.